Regents, Reformers, and Revolutionaries: Indonesian Voices of Colonial Days

Asian Studies at Hawaii, No. 21

Regents, Reformers, and Revolutionaries: Indonesian Voices of Colonial Days
Selected Historical Readings 1899-1949

Translated, edited, and annotated by Greta O. Wilson

Asian Studies Program
University of Hawaii
THE UNIVERSITY PRESS OF HAWAII

Copyright © 1978 by Greta O. Wilson
All rights reserved
Manufactured in the United States of America

Library of Congress Cataloging in Publication Data
Main entry under title:

Regents, reformers, and revolutionaries.

  (Asian studies at Hawaii; no. 21)
  Translated from Dutch and Indonesian.
  Bibliography: p.
  Includes index.
  1. Indonesia—History—20th century—Addresses, essays, lectures. I. Wilson, Greta O., 1928–
II. Series.
DS3.A2A82 no. 21 [DS643] 959.8'03   77-20686

Contents

Illustrations	vii
Acknowledgments	ix
Abbreviations	xi
Introduction	xiii
PART I. THE REGENTS	1
Pangeran Ario Hadiningrat: A JAVANESE PIONEER (1847–1915)	3
The Decline of the Prestige of the Native Rulers (1899)	6
P. A. Achmad Djajadiningrat: A WESTERNIZED ARISTOCRAT (1877–1943)	17
Editor's Introduction: Development and Demise of the Sarekat Islam	21
The Sarekat Islam (1936)	22
Editor's Introduction: Regency Councils	27
The Position of the Regents on Java and Madura in the Present Administrative System (1929)	28
PART II. THE REFORMERS	43
W. K. Tehupeiory: AMBONESE SPOKESMAN FOR THE NEW ELITE (1883–1946)	45
Editor's Introduction: In Defense of the School for Indonesian Physicians	47
The Native Physicians (1908)	48

H. A. Salim: MODERN MOSLEM (1884–1954) — 61
Editor's Introduction: The League of Young Moslems — 65
The Veiling and Isolation of Women (1926) — 66
Editor's Introduction: Coolie Legislation and the Penal Sanction — 73
Coolie Legislation and the Penal Sanction (1923) — 74

M. H. Thamrin: PRAGMATIC POLITICIAN (1894–1941) — 83
Editor's Introduction: A Nationalist Party in the People's Council — 87
Announcing the Formation of the Nationalist Faction (1930) — 88
Editor's Introduction: The Fate of the Sutardjo Petition — 99
The Sutardjo Petition (1936) — 100
Editor's Introduction: Toward Racial Integration — 103
Proposal for Equal Pay for Soldiers Regardless of Race (1940) — 104

Mohammad Natsir: PALADIN AND PATRIOT (Born 1908) — 109
Editor's Introduction: The Quest for Education — 111
Our Educational System Lacks Teachers (1938) — 112
Editor's Introduction: Political Concerns of the Early Forties — 117
The Political Standpoint of M. H. Thamrin (1941) — 118
Is There "Wang Ching-wei-ism" in Indonesia? "No!" We Respond (1941) — 123

PART III. THE REVOLUTIONARIES — 127

Mohammad Hatta: SCHOLAR AND STATESMAN (Born 1902) — 129
Editor's Introduction: An Advocate of Noncooperation — 133
Manifest Cooperation (1929) — 134
Editor's Introduction: A Nationalist Comments on an "Ethical" Governor-General — 137
Governor-General de Graeff and the Indonesian Independence Movement (n.d.) — 138
Editor's Introduction: The Round Table Conference — 149
Toward the Transfer of Sovereignty (1949) — 150

Ir. Sukarno: UNIFIER OF A THOUSAND ISLANDS (1901–1970) — 159
Toward a Brown Front (1927) — 161
Can Non-Cooperation Not Bring about Mass Action and Power Formation? (1933) — 165

L. N. Palar: SOCIALIST AND DIPLOMAT (Born 1902)	175
Editor's Introduction: The Linggadjati Agreement	179
A Brief for Indonesia's Independence (1947)	181
Glossary	193
Suggested Reading	195
Index	197

Illustrations

Sixth International Congress of Historians of Asia, Jogjakarta, Indonesia, August, 1974	viii
Pangeran Ario Hadiningrat	2
Pangeran Achmad Djajadiningrat	16
Hadji Agus Salim	60
M. H. Thamrin	84
Mohammad Natsir	108
Dr. Mohammad Hatta	128
Sukarno	158
L. N. Palar	174

Acknowledgments

The impetus to compile an anthology of selected Indonesian historical readings came, unwittingly, from an East Asia specialist, Professor Chalmers A. Johnson. While auditing his undergraduate course on modern Japan and China at the University of California at Berkeley I realized that, while sufficient source material by East Asians in translation is extant, what Indonesians have written (often in Dutch) during the colonial era is little known. Available texts on Indonesian history and the monographs published on a myriad of subjects are invariably the work of non-Indonesians.

After I decided that an anthology was in order, I discussed my plan with Professor Harry J. Benda at the convention of the Association for Asian Studies in Washington in 1971. He was enthusiastic and offered to be my coworker, cautioning that no financial assistance might be available. He proved to be correct. Nonetheless, I felt that my time and efforts were well spent if this collection of selected readings by Indonesians promoted a better understanding of their country, where I was born and had lived for eighteen years.

The lack of financial assistance made it imperative to use articles or published materials easily accessible in American libraries or readily securable from the Netherlands. The guiding principle in making the selections was to have various ethnic groups represented dealing with divers subjects. The preface outlines the historical background from 1899 until 1949. All of the selections have been annotated, and a short biographical sketch of each author has been included. This collection is primarily intended as a supplement to historical texts on Indonesia for the benefit of those who are unable to read Dutch.

My work would have been well-nigh impossible if I had not received the assistance of several librarians. First, I would like to thank members of the interlibrary loan service of the University of California at Berkeley for their swift and very able cooperation in securing material needed for my research. Thanks are also due the interlibrary loan service at Cornell for providing me with copies of articles and other data indispensable to my work.

Mr. R. J. P. van Hoorn of the Royal Institute of Anthropology and Linguistics in Leyden, the Netherlands, has rendered many services far beyond the call of duty, such as locating articles and supplying much needed information. I would like to express my sincere thanks for his help. My gratitude too, to Mr. A. Kohar Rony of the Library of Congress who gave me his advice and assistance during my brief stay in Washington, D. C. I have also benefited from the advice and suggestions of Professor Daniel S. Lev of the University of Washington, Professor Paul van der Veur of Ohio University at Athens, and especially of Abdurrachman Surjomihardjo of LIPI in Jakarta. The late Harry Benda, who was my teacher at Yale, offered to assist me with my work. His untimely death restricted his actual contribution toward improving my translation of Hadiningrat's article. But his advice, suggestions, and comments on the "art of translating"—based on his own considerable experience—were invaluable to me.

Mr. Peter Ananda, Southeast Asia Bibliographer at the University of California at Berkeley, deserves special recognition for assisting me, at very short notice, with my translation, from Indonesian into English, of Sukarno's article on noncooperation. He also translated the greater part of the articles by M. Natsir.

Without the assistance of Professor Walter F. Vella of the University of Hawaii and Professor Harry J. Lamley, chairman of the Asian Studies Publications Committee, of the University of Hawaii, this collection might never have been published. I wish to thank both men for their support and cooperation.

Two of the authors kindly extended permission to translate: Dr. Mohammad Hatta and Mr. Mohammad Natsir. The latter furnished me with biographical data that I had requested. The publisher of *Djedjak Langkah Hadji Agus Salim,* Tintamas in Jakarta, allowed me to include two of the late H. A. Salim's articles.

My husband Terry and my three daughters Emily, Bonnie, and Trixie have given me considerable help and encouragement during the preparation of this work. But I alone am responsible for the anthology in its entirety.

Greta O. Wilson
Diablo, California

Abbreviations

AMS	Algemene Middelbare School, a high school which was an extension of junior high schoool. Its diploma had the same value as that of a HBS, which is directly connected with grade school.
BB	Binnenlandsch Bestuur, Dutch civil administration
BFO	Bijeenkomst Federaal Overleg, Assembly for Federal Consultation
BU	Budi Utomo, Noble Endeavor, an organization founded in 1908
Drs.	Academic title indicating that the person has completed all requirements for a doctorate except the dissertation.
GAPI	Gabungan Politik Indonesia, Indonesian Political Association
GG	Governor-general
HBS	Hogere Burger School, a high school
H.I.K.	Hollandsch Inlandsche Kweekschool, Dutch Indonesian Teachers' Training School
H.I.S.	Hollands Inlandse School
Ir.	Ingenieur, a degree in engineering
JIB	Jong Islamieten Bond, League of Young Moslems
KNIL	Koninklijk Nederlands Indisch Leger, Royal Dutcheast Indies Army
KPM	Koninklijke Paketvaart Maatschappij, Royal Shipping Company
Masjumi	Madjelis Sjuro Muslimin Indonesia, Association of Indonesian Moslems
MULO	Meer Uitgebreid Lager Onderwijs, a sort of junior high school
PNI	Partai Nasional Indonesia, Indonesian National Party
PPPKI	Permufakatan Perhimpunan Politik Kebangsaan Indonesia, Consensus of Political Associations of Indonesia
PSI	Partai Sosialis Indonesia, Indonesian Socialist Party
PUTERA	Pusat Tenaga Rakjat, Center of the People's Strength, founded in 1943 under the aegis of the Japanese occupation forces to mobilize Indonesian forces
RTC	Round Table Conference
SI	Sarekat Islam, Islamic Organization
STOVIA	School voor Opleiding van Inlandse Artsen, School for Training of Indonesian Physicians
TRI	Tentara Republik Indonesia, Indonesian Republican Army

Sixth International Congress of Historians of Asia, Jogjakarta, Indonesia, August, 1974. Left to right: Dr. Mohammad Hatta, former Vice President of the Republic of Indonesia; Dr. Paramita Abdurrachaman, historian, LIPI, Jakarta; Greta Wilson, speaker on the panel "Leaders of Modern Asia."

Introduction

Although Dutch rule in Indonesia purportedly lasted three hundred years, it was not until the early years of the twentieth century that the Dutch could claim complete control over the archipelago. Late in the sixteenth century, Dutch traders arrived in the spice islands, and a trading post was established in West Java, in the early part of the seventeenth century. For about two hundred years the Dutch presence was primarily confined to Java and the Moluccas.

The Dutch East India Company, founded in 1602, was taken over by the Dutch government in 1799; the war in Europe prevented the inauguration of a consistent policy for the area under Dutch control. Not until after the Java War (1825–1830) was a concerted effort made to exploit the colony. Effective development of the islands' resources by Dutch entrepreneurs necessitated political control and gradually the native rulers were brought under the "protection" of the Kingdom of the Netherlands. All hostile regions, Achin in North Sumatra in particular, were subjugated—a process not accomplished until 1904.

Not all Dutchmen agreed that economic exploitation was beneficial to the peoples of Indonesia. Many voices were raised in protest, culminating in a formal change of colonial policy with the enunciation of the ethical policy by the Dutch queen.

Three paragraphs of the address at the opening of Parliament in September 1901 were devoted to Holland's faraway Southeast Asian possession. The Dutch government had the duty, as a Christian power " . . . to permeate the whole administration with the notion that the Netherlands has to fulfill an ethical mission in these regions . . . . "[1]

Thirty years earlier, a young Javanese aristocrat named Hadiningrat, who later became Regent of Demak, had already suggested that the Dutch had a task to fulfill in elevating the Indonesian people.[2] The time was not yet ripe, but two decades later the colonial administration requested that Hadiningrat submit a memorandum on the cause of the waning prestige of the native rulers.[3] His advice influenced Dutch policy and officials, in particular, the Islamic scholar and Adviser for Native Affairs, Christian Snouck Hurgronje.[4]

One of the earliest Indonesian attempts to raise the national consciousness came with the establishment of Budi Utomo (Noble Endeavor) in 1908. One of the initiators was Raden Sutomo, at that time a student at the School for Training of Native Physicians (STOVIA).[5] Budi Utomo was not a formal political organization but rather limited itself to seeking expanded educational opportunities and to raising the general level of the Javanese people. Its influence on the population was insignificant.

Between 1910 and 1930 the number of political groups multiplied. In 1912 the Indische Partij (Indies party) was formed by Dr. Tjipto Mangunkusumo, a graduate of STOVIA,[6] Suwardi Surjaningrat,[7] a dropout of the same school and E. F. E. Douwes Dekker, a Eurasian. Because of its revolutionary program—its founders openly advocated independence—the colonial government refused recognition to this group and banished its Indonesian leaders.[8]

Another party established in 1912, the Sarekat Islam (Islamic Organization),[9] had as its aim the promotion of a better understanding of Islam thereby raising the national consciousness. Although it enjoyed great popularity for a while, attempts by communist members to take over leadership led to its decline and reorganization.

Leadership in the drive for a national awakening did not emanate from the native administrators, the regents, but from the recipients of western education, graduates of STOVIA, the school for native officials (OSVIA), and the Dutch high schools (HBS), who had nothing to gain by the perpetuation of the declining power of the traditional elite. Many entered government service and, because of racial discrimination coupled with low pay and prestige, became aware of the humiliating status of being colonized. Throughout the colonial period the demand for more and better education, the fight against race discrimination, and for amelioration of the economic conditions of the Indonesian people continued unabated but was largely ignored.[10]

The twenties saw the decline of the ethical policy. Neither the Dutch nor the Indonesians were satisfied with its effectiveness or results. Dutch colonial policy, always heavily influenced by the result of elections in the Netherlands, brought a swing to the right: a conservative Minister of

Colonies, Simon de Graaff, and a governor-general, Dirk Fock, who had no sympathy for nor understanding of nationalist aspirations.

Although the ethical policy had envisaged administrative decentralization, the powers conferred upon local and regional councils and the national council—People's Council (Volksraad)—all fell far short of expectations. Many native administrators considered these representative bodies a further encroachment upon their prestige,[11] whereas the nationalists felt that, shorn of any real powers, these councils were but a colonial hoax.

Concessions, prompted by rumors of a leftist takeover in the Netherlands, were promised by a jittery Governor-General van Limburg Stirum in 1918 to grant the People's Council cogoverning powers but were rescinded. An Indonesian majority of the council, which had been the goal at its inception, did not become a reality until the early thirties. The concerted efforts of Indonesians of such diverse political persuasions as Mohammad Husni Thamrin, a council member since 1927, and Achmad Djajadiningrat, the regent of Batavia, brought about the long-awaited majority.

At the outset the council had attracted such members as the Minangkabau physician Abdul Rivai and the Moslem scholar Hadji Agus Salim, but had failed to gain the support of the younger, far more militant intellectuals. Mohammad Hatta,[12] son of a Minangkabau religious leader, who in the twenties and early thirties was a student in the Netherlands, and Ir. Sukarno,[13] a graduate of the Bandung Technical College, openly advocated independence and noncooperation with the colonial ruler.

Communist instigated uprisings in 1926–1927 in Sumatra's West Coast and West Java (Banten) together with incendiary speeches by militant nationalists sowed terror in the hearts of a large part of the Dutch colonists. Although Governor-General de Graeff, sympathetic toward the nationalist cause, for a while was able to withstand pressures for action from this segment of the population, rumors that a revolution was imminent led to the arrest of Sukarno, who was considered the chief instigator. Despite vigorous protests by Indonesian members of the People's Council[14] who were led by Sukarno's friend Thamrin, Sukarno was convicted. But he was released by de Graeff before his sentence expired. Governor-General de Jonghe, who succeeded de Graeff in 1931, had no qualms whatever in exerting his extensive powers; and in rapid succession the most outspoken nationalists—Sukarno, Hatta and Sutan Sjahrir—were arrested, incarcerated, and banished to outlying islands in the archipelago. Indonesian members of the People's Council who enjoyed parliamentary immunity escaped arrest but were unable to reverse the policies adopted.

In 1936, a council member and native official, Sutardjo Djojohadikusumo, proposed to convene an imperial conference to discuss the status of the Indies, and introduced a petition seeking autonomy for Indonesia within ten years. Although the Sutardjo Petition, as it became known, was accepted by the People's Council in September 1936, the decisive majority support came from the Eurasian members. The Dutch Parliament rejected it more than two years later.[15]

The action to win the support of the Indonesian people for the petition made Hadji Agus Salim move to abandon his stand of noncooperation with the colonial government, and he became active in the nationalist movement once again. M. H. Thamrin, after Sukarno's arrest in 1933, became one of the principal spokesmen for the nationalist cause, both within and without the council. He threw the support of his political group within the council behind the Sutardjo Petition and traveled far and wide over the archipelago in search of popular backing. After the petition was rejected he called for a federation of nationalist groups in an effort to persuade the colonial government to grant concessions, and then later called for the formation of an Indonesian parliament. His arrest and sudden death in January 1941—still shrouded in mystery—removed this astute nationalist forever from the political scene. But the Indonesians relentlessly pursued and pressured for more participation in the governance of their country.[16]

Governor-General Tjarda van Starkenborgh Stachouwer, de Jonghe's replacement in 1936, had a policy toward the demands of the nationalists that was vacillating.[17] Whether he personally favored more participation by Indonesians in their own affairs is not yet known, but there is little doubt that his actions were severely curtailed by a conservative administration in the Netherlands that was wholly unwilling to contemplate granting concessions.[18] This group remained in power until March 1942.

The approaching Japanese menace led the colonial government, early in 1942, to seek the support of M. Hatta in return for his freedom. He was brought back to Java but refused to abandon his stand on noncooperation. Sukarno remained a prisoner until June 1942, when the Japanese were well established in the archipelago.

The Japanese interregnum (March 1942 until September 1945—when British troops landed in Java) heralded the demise of Dutch rule. The Dutch returned to Indonesia in November 1945, and the Indonesians led by Sukarno and Hatta, proclaimed their independence on August 17, 1945, and fought a heroic five-year struggle against the far better-equipped Dutch military forces.[19] In December 1949 they finally won independence from their colonial masters, who had to bow to overwhelming international support for Indonesia's cause.[20]

INTRODUCTION

The transition from subjugation to sovereignty was a process spanning several decades and was wrought by Indonesians of varied social and cultural backgrounds: aristocrat and commoner, Minangkabau and Batak, Javanese and Sundanese, Menadonese and Ambonese—nationalists all.

Bhinneka tunggal ika,[21] unity in diversity, the motto of the Indonesian republic, quite befits the nine authors whose work is represented here. Notwithstanding their diversity in ethnic origin, background, training, they had at least one characteristic in common: they spoke for change.

The tool for becoming an effective spokesman was provided by western training; each one of these writers was well educated. Pangeran Ario Hadiningrat received his basic instruction from a private Dutch tutor and was subsequently self-taught. Dr. W. K. Tehupeiory and Ir. Sukarno both had professional degrees—in medicine and engineering respectively. Dr. Mohammad Hatta has an advanced degree in political economics. The five others received at least a Dutch high school education, which is equivalent of two years of good U. S. college training. L. N. Palar has an additional two years of higher education, and Mohammad Natsir a diploma from a teachers' training school.

Dutch high schools offered mandatory courses in the natural sciences, the social sciences, and four to five years of training in four western languages. Thus the Indonesian graduates of these schools, in addition to their native tongue, read and spoke Dutch, French, German, and English. Mohammad Natsir—as was the late Hadji Agus Salim—is proficient also in Arabic.

The ability to write and speak Dutch was imperative because the plea for reform was directed toward the alien, colonial ruler. Sometimes, when the appeal came from the regents, without whose support the colonial policy of *divide et impera* would have collapsed, the Dutch made an effort to comply. Thus Hadiningrat's advice and his request for better education, particularly for the sons of native administrators, was slowly and incompletely heeded. But the result of these concessions, more western education for a larger number of Indonesians, contributed to a large extent to the emergence of the nationalist movement.

The movement's spokesmen, writing in Dutch, did not necessarily direct themselves to the colonial ruler. Mohammad Hatta, writing from the Netherlands, addressed himself primarily to the movement in Indonesia. The articles of Hadji Agus Salim and M. Natsir on Islam were decidedly not exclusively, if at all, intended for the foreign dominators.

By the late 1920s the use of Indonesian (derived from Malay, long the lingua franca in the archipelago) by the nationalists, became more widespread. Concomitantly the use of the words Indonesian (for Inlander[22]) and Indonesia (for Netherlands Indies) became basic to the nationalist cause. This culminated in the 1940 session of the People's Council,[23] in Thamrin's motion requesting that the use of these words become official.[24]

Employing Indonesian in addressing the colonial masters did not have the effect hoped for. When Thamrin, in July 1938,[25] grandiloquently announced to the People's Council that his political group would henceforth exclusively use Indonesian, he might well have satisfied a sense of national pride, but he and his cohorts quickly discovered that they were literally talking to the walls of the council building. Well-nigh all of the Dutch members were completely unable to comprehend them. The Dutch schools in the archipelago with all their excellence in education did not—at any level—provide courses in the indigenous languages.

The desire for change common to this heterogeneous group of spokesmen differed only in scope. They all wanted a share of the political power, and they all sought equal rights with the colonial rulers even, at the outset, the revolutionaries. The regents envisaged primarily enhancement or bolstering of their own status. The reformers' goals were multifarious: to improve the lot of the coolies, to equalize the pay of soldiers, to upgrade the status of the native physicians, and to enlarge educational opportunities. The revolutionaries were bolder; they wanted total change in the structure of government and were willing and ready to assist in the forceful overthrow of the established rule.

The lines drawn between the three groups are admittedly somewhat arbitrary. M. H. Thamrin, if indeed as is alleged, made plans with the Japanese to establish a new order in Indonesia and would qualify as a bona fide revolutionary.

With all its negative effects colonialism brought to the fore an astonishingly large group of great men of which this selection gives but a sampling.

NOTES

1. The paragraphs read:
   "As a Christian power, the Netherlands has a duty to improve the legal position of the native Christians in the Indian archipelago, to lend the Christian missions more support, and to permeate the whole administration with the notion that the Netherlands has to fulfill an ethical mission in these regions.
   In this regard of special interest to me is the declining prosperity of the native population in Java. The causes of this I wish to investigate. Regulations to protect the contract coolies will be strictly observed. Decentralization of the administration will be promoted.
   I trust that the situation in the northern part of Sumatra, when current policy is adhered to, will lead ere long to total pacification."
   E. N. van Raalte, ed., *Troonredes, Openingsredes, Inhuldigingsredes, 1814–1963* (The Hague: Staatsdrukkerij, 1964), p. 194.

INTRODUCTION   xix

2.   In 1871 Hadiningrat submitted a memorandum to the Director of Internal Affairs (Binnenlandsch Bestuur). See p. 12 herein.
3.   Although the advice was written in 1896, it was not published until 1899.
4.   Snouck advocated to extend western education to the sons of high officials, thus ensuring the support of this group. C. Snouck Hurgronje. *Verspreide Geschriften* (Leipzig: Schroeder, 1924), vol. 4, no. 2, p. 296.
5.   For a detailed discussion of the medical school and its precursor, the School for Doktor Djawa (the school for medical assistants), see W. K. Tehupeiory, "The Native Physicians," pp. 48–59.
6.   Dr. Tjipto was decorated by the colonial government for his work done among cholera patients during an epidemic. He later returned his decoration and became a vociferous critic not only of the colonial ruler but also of the traditional elite, the regents whose support made Dutch rule effective.
7.   Suwardi Surjaningrat was a member of the Royal House of Paku Alam (in Central Java). After his exile in the Netherlands he returned to Java, changed his name to Ki Hadjar Dewantoro, and became the founder of the Taman Siswa schools, which advocated an educational system founded upon a synthesis of western and indigenous cultures.
8.   As a Eurasian Douwes Dekker could not be exiled. Later the colonial government displayed less compunction in observing the rule of law and the protection of its citizens' civil rights. After the arrest of Thamrin in 1941, Douwes Dekker was arrested and exiled to Surinam, at that time a Dutch colony.
9.   See Djajadiningrat's article on the Sarekat Islam, pp. 22–25.
10. Natsir's article on education "Our Educational System Lacks Teachers," pp. 112–115; Thamrin's speech to the People's Council, "Proposal for Equal Pay for All Soldiers Regardless of Race," pp. 104–107; the introductory note to Salim's speech "Coolie Legislation and the Penal Sanction," p. 74 and his remarks to the People's Council, pp. 74–81 describe the economic exploitation on the plantations and the economic plight of the people in general.
11. Djajadiningrat in his article, "The Position of the Regents on Java and Madura in the Present Administrative System," pp. 28–42, gives an excellent account of the powers of the regency council and of its chairman, the regent.
12. Hatta's view on noncooperation appears in his "Manifest Cooperation," pp. 134–136 and his "Governor-General de Graeff and the Indonesian Nationalist Movement," pp. 138–147.
13. Sukarno's view on noncooperation appears in "Can Noncooperation Not Lead to Mass Action and Power Formation?" pp 165–172.
14. Thamrin's speech in the People's Council, "Announcing the Formation of the Nationalist Faction," pp. 88–96 describes vividly the actions the colonial government had taken to suppress the outspoken nationalists.
15. For a background of the Sutardjo Petition and Thamrin's council speech see "The Sutardjo Petition," p. 100.
16. Mohammad Natsir discussed Thamrin's political views in "The Political Standpoint of M. H. Thamrin," pp. 118–122; and Indonesia's concerns in "Is There Wang-Ching-weiism' in Indonesia? 'No!' We Respond," pp. 123–125.
17. Tjarda's perennial, bland smile resembling a billboard advertisement for toothpaste, earned him the nickname "Tuan Tanpasta" (Mr. Toothpaste) by the Indonesians.
18. Exemplified by such men as Prime Minister Colijn and—sometime—Minister of Colonies, Welter.

19. Mohammad Hatta, "Toward the Transfer of Sovereignty," pp. 150-156, poignantly describes Indonesia's struggle against the Dutch. For the role that the United Nations played see, Alastair M. Taylor, *Indonesian Independence and the United Nations* (Ithaca: Cornell University Press, 1960).
20. L. N. Palar in "A Brief for Indonesia's Independence," analyzes Dutch sentiment about the Indonesian revolution. The speech was made to the Dutch lower house, Tweede Kamer, of which Palar was a member at that time, pp. 181-191.
21. Old Javanese.
22. See note 9, p. 157.
23. People's Council, founded in 1918 was a quasi-representative body, consisting of members partly appointed and partly elected. For powers of the council, see note 4, p. 97 for its composition, note 2, p. 148.
24. See p. 122, note 7.
25. Speech made in the People's Council, July 12, 1938. Although most members of the *Fraksi Nasional* used Indonesian often, after Thamrin gave his speech, Dutch was still frequently resorted to even by Thamrin himself. See pp. 104-107 infra.

**PART I
THE REGENTS**

Pangeran Ario Hadiningrat. Courtesy of Arsip Nasional Indonesia

Pangeran Ario Hadiningrat: A Javanese Pioneer[1] (1847–1915)

To Pangeran Ario Hadiningrat, outspoken Regent of Demak, the decline of the prestige of the Javanese rulers was caused by their low educational level.[2] As a remedy he proposed more and better schools and thus provided the first concrete plan by an Indonesian to elevate the people.

Hadiningrat was born July 14, 1847, the son of Pangeran Ario Tjondronegoro, Regent of Demak, a very enlightened man who, aware of the importance of western education, secured a private Dutch tutor (C. E. van Kesteren, later editor of the *Indische Gids*) for his four sons.[3] Three of them became regents: Raden Mas Adipati Tjondronegoro of Kudus and later Brèbès; Raden Mas Ario Sosroningrat, Raden Adjeng Kartini's father, of Japara; and Pangeran Ario Hadiningrat of Demak.

Hadiningrat started his career in the native administration as a writer and became *djaksa* in 1871 and *hoofddjaksa* in 1872. His abilities and his perfect command of Dutch brought him to the attention of a member of the Council of the Indies (the advisory body to the governor-general) who made him his assistant and took him on a mission to Sumatra to study the legal system.

In 1881 Hadiningrat succeeded his father as Regent of Demak. (Demak is situated on the northeastern part of Central Java.) It was an area poor in resources and frequently affected by natural catastrophes: floods, droughts, and sandstorms. Hadiningrat performed his task as regent conscientiously and unfailingly sought to alleviate the plight of the population. His regency was one of the first to set up *lumbung desa* (granaries stocked with rice which was loaned against low interest rates in the form of produce). He secured government loans to purchase water buffaloes, to plant coconut gardens, and to grow cassava. He encouraged the peasants to intensify the cultivation of their rice fields and, with justification, can be called a highly capable, enterprising, forward-looking man.

Hadiningrat also served the government well. He was a member of two commissions, one studying the declining prosperity in Java and the other, administrative reforms. During the last years of his life he was a member of the provincial council of Central Java.

Although admired by many Dutchmen who befriended him, there were at least an equal number who found Hadiningrat obnoxious, stubborn, haughty, and unapproachable. He was very much aware of the legal rights accompanying his position and would not tolerate any encroachment upon his authority. It is not surprising that Demak was not considered a choice assignment among Dutch officials.

But the colonial ruler valued Hadiningrat's counsel, and his advice influenced colonial policy and the recommendations of those who served the government, for example, C. Snouck Hurgronje.[4] Hadiningrat's proposal, in fact, may be regarded a precursor to the Ethical Policy. Some parts of it may appear paternalistic to the modern reader, and in many respects his attitude toward the inlander does not differ fundamentally from that of the alien ruler to whom he appropriately suggested improvement in the status of the elite.

As Hadiningrat had predicted education transformed Indonesian society, but the prestige of the traditional elite was never restored. On the contrary, when the colonial power slowly, hesitatingly, and very meagerly enlarged educational opportunities for Indonesians, leadership fell to the lower ranks of the Javanese aristocracy and the upcoming commercial class of Sumatra's West Coast. These groups provided the foremen of the Indonesian nationalist movement.

Hadiningrat was a pioneer in his day, a man who discerned with acuity the declining power of the high aristocracy and correctly assessed the eroding changes colonialism had wrought. He was neither a democrat nor a nationalist; in the archipelago at that time, nationalism had not yet emerged. But his advice benefited those who later carried the banner for Indonesia's independence. Regrettably, he is now forgotten. One will search in vain for his name in the *Ensiklopedia Indonesia*.

NOTES

1. The title and much of the information in this sketch have been derived from C. J. Hasselman "Pangeran Ario Hadiningrat, Een Javaansch Pioneer," *De Gids*, vol. 79, no. 3, 1915, pp. 249-300; some data was taken from *Encyclopeadie van Nederlandsch-Indie*, 2:4, and *De Indische Mercuur*, 1915, no. 38, p. 253.

2. The title Pangeran either denotes a member of the royal family or is bestowed by the government for exceptional services. Here it is a bestowed title. Ario is an additional title not existing alone. See L. M. C. van den Berg, *De Inlandsche Rangen en Titles op Java en Madoera* (Batavia: Landsdrukkerij, 1887), pp. 2-3.
3. C. Th. van Deventer mentions that there were five sons. *Leven en Arbeid van Mr. C. Th. van Deventer,* H. T. Colenbrander en J. E. Stokvis, eds. (Amsterdam: van Kampen, 1916), vol. 2, p. 310.
4. C. Snouck Hurgronje, *Verspreide Geschriften,* vol. 4, no. 2 (Leipzig: Schroeder, 1924), p. 296. C. Snouck Hurgronje was Advisor for Native Affairs from 1889 until 1906.

The Decline of the Prestige of the Native Rulers and Ways to Effectuate Changes in This Condition

Some time ago, in 1893, a statement was made in the Second Chamber [the Lower House of the Dutch Parliament] that the prestige of the Native rulers[1] was no longer what it had been, and subsequently the colonial government investigated the truth of this statement and what could be done to improve the situation.

Whereas previously, especially at the time of the cultivation system,[2] the cooperation of the Native rulers was very much needed and the administration was virtually conducted through their intercession, later policies often entailed that the European administration directly contact the population, bypassing the Native rulers. Moreover, there was a tendency to raise the level of individual consciousness of the Natives.

The introduction of these policies created increasing demands for better educated European officials, but generally the level of education of the Native rulers remained unchanged, another reason Native officials were and are no longer consulted on a variety of important matters, which naturally further weakened their status and prestige.

In my humble opinion this is a situation which cannot be reversed easily, for no one desires a return to the old ways. Improvement under the

This memorandum was submitted to the colonial government at the request of Governor-General Jonkheer C. H. J. van der Wijck in 1896. It was published, in slightly abbreviated form, at the initiative of C. J. Hasselman, a friend of Hadiningrat's, *"De achteruitgang van het prestige der inlandsche hoofden en de middelen om daarin verbetering te brengen,"* in Tijdschriftvoor het Binnenlandsch Bestuur, Part 17 (1899), pp. 367-385.

present conditions, however, can be expected, but only if Native officials are first of all given an education and imbued with a new ethos.

Many ascribe the decline of their authority to changing times, but in my opinion the rulers also owe it primarily to themselves if they are less often consulted than was previously the case . . . .

Although the chiefs, because of their position and frequent contacts with the Europeans, appear to stand on a somewhat higher level, they are in many respects not in a much better position than the common people.

One of my acquaintances, at that time consul in Jidda,[3] wrote me that he was annoyed by the way the pilgrims from Java allowed themselves to be swindled.

His letter continued:

> The Arabs here do not cheat the Egyptian, Persian, Afghan, Syrian, Tunisian, Moroccan or British-Indian pilgrims; the Arabs have a respectful fear of all of them, for they would not accept such treatment. These people are suspicious of anything the Arabs say, while the very opposite can be observed in our pilgrims; they unconditionally accept an Arab's word as the truth and an expression of unselfishness. In fact, the Turkish Governor of Jidda even remarked that the *hadji*s from Java are meeker than sheep.

This letter adequately illustrates how submissive the Natives are in some respects.

Most certainly their rulers are somewhat better, for in their frequent contact with Europeans they have seen, heard, and experienced more. . . . Indeed, we find among the younger generation some who have received training at the schools for Native officials[4] or at the high schools, but their number is as yet insignificant.

The majority of rulers have learned to read and write either from their parents or from relatives and acquaintances, or they have completed a few grades of the public school for Natives.

But even the number of officials who have successfully completed this kind of schooling is as yet so small that it cannot compare favorably with the number of existing schools.[5]

Not surprisingly their intellectual development stands, as a rule, on a very low level compared to that of the Europeans. In particular, considering the stringent requirements imposed on specialists and junior officials.

Because of this great difference in education the Native officials are pushed into the background. On the whole they do little more than carry out given orders; they are no more than *mandurs*.

Their culture and learning are no longer in conformity with present conditions, and as a result, the Europeans in general regard them as inferior in all respects and adopt a more or less supercilious or somewhat indifferent attitude toward them. . . .

Besides, the Javanese condones and endures a great deal and is resigned to his lot, either because of unfounded fear for future troubles or because of his fatalistic conditioning, therefore we need not look far for the cause of the decline of the prestige of the Native officials.

I shall now examine why the general level of education of the Natives has remained stagnant.

First, one must not forget that for centuries Europeans have persistently striven for progress. This restless drive alone is sufficient to make the Javanese, who has remained stationary, fall far behind. More than that Europeans will not leave a stone unturned to further their advancement. To name an example, they cannot expect to be recognized as specialists in their field or be appointed as public servants unless they meet specific requirements as far as ability and aptitude are concerned . . . .

Taking into consideration that European education has improved considerably in the past years and that additional efforts are continually made to advance and expand education so that everyone has ample opportunity to acquire training, it is obvious that the educational level of the Europeans is bound to advance enormously.

For the Native, however, the situation is totally different.

Scholars have not yet agreed on the efficacy of the Native grade schools. For prospective Native officials, it is true, we do have on this island three so-called schools for chiefs but enrollment is limited,[6] it is left entirely up to each individual to determine whether he will take the opportunity to acquire training in these schools.

Many parents do not deem training for their sons as necessary, for it still happens everyday that *magangs* who have had no schooling are accepted into the public service. Why, then, go to all the trouble and expense?

Besides, even if concerned parents may like to take advantage of educational opportunities for their children, their desires may remain just that, for admission to the schools, after all, is restricted.

Therefore the number of those graduating from the schools for Native chiefs each year is insufficient to meet the demand for new officials, and vacancies are invariably filled by *magangs*.

The level of schooling of this category of people will be indicated below . . . . As far as the older ones are concerned . . . they were primarily recruited from *magangs* who worked in private business concerns and who never received any education to speak of. With few exceptions they can only read and write and hardly know arithmetic.

But even if all *magangs* had successfully completed the Native school, one can never expect much of them. The school's curriculum is such that its graduates may well be quite competent to become *desa* heads or scribes, but the curriculum is quite inadequate to meet the high requirements nowadays placed on district officials . . . . [7]

In general the treatment accorded the Natives by the alien ruler is far from bad, albeit somewhat condescending and not conducive to generate close relationships. This happens quite frequently as the Native lacks the courage to request explanations where necessary. As a rule he is resigned to whatever he is ordered to do . . . .

Even Native rulers, at times, experience less than acceptable treatment from Europeans. And they, too, acquiesce, partly because they fear they will not be listened to, but also partly because they have their own reasons for complying. Not only Dutch private citizens, but Dutch officials as well are occasionally guilty of such disrespectful behavior, even though it is their duty to counteract it. Whatever the reasons, these actions must have an adverse effect on the prestige of the rulers . . . .

But not all aliens are guilty of unseemly behavior toward the Natives, nor can all those guilty of such behavior be held accountable.

. . . . If they do act improperly toward the dominated, this is often caused by clumsiness or ignorance of local customs and habits, or, because they see other Dutch officials act similarly, with impunity.

Nevertheless, the population sees and experiences the bad treatment and draws its own conclusions. One of the oft-mentioned grievances is treating all Natives, regardless of rank or class, in a similar manner. Just to mention a minor point, for instance, there is the habit of addressing Native rulers, whether in official capacity or in daily contact, in low Javanese regardless of status or age—even by young and lower-ranking officials—something that violates accepted customs.[8]

The Native official of low birth sees this as a leveling of classes, but the conclusion the population draws goes further; they regard such treatment as a humiliation of the aristocracy, and this does not reflect favorably on the prestige of the Native official in general and on the authority of those of high birth in particular.

Some also attribute the decline of their prestige to changed times, prompting Dutch officials, in many cases, to establish direct contact with the population and bypassing its chiefs . . . . It is not always easy to draw the proper line between what, indeed, can be communicated to the population directly and what requires the cooperation of the rulers. Wherever Native chiefs demonstrate unfitness for a given task or sound reasons exist not to heed their advice, it is in my opinion justified to bypass them, but even then only in matters in which they have no understanding or which need to be discharged without them . . . .

... it has happened more than once that in appointing Regents, in cases where the provisions governing such appointments are not applicable, far less attention has been paid to the family background of the appointee; this invariably provides the Natives with opportunities to indulge in conjectures which are unpleasant to those of high birth.

To enhance the new office holder's status, the government ennobles him at the time of his appointment. This invariably does not accomplish the goal, for the Natives value birth more than titles ....

I am all in favor of showing the Native that, in accordance with fairness and justice, commoners can be placed in a position of attaining the highest office in our administration as a result of knowledge, diligence, and devotion to duty. But I do not deem it advisable to elevate many nonaristocrats to high positions, a practice that still violates Native concepts; for the Native still lacks the opportunity to obtain an education or to distinguish himself through years of service.

In the past, Native princes occasionally elevated commoners to the nobility, but although arbitrariness prevailed, as a rule this only occurred in exceptional cases.

To avoid tensions, far-reaching changes violating *adat* and accepted customs must be accompanied by an increase in education of the dominated.

In my opinion, the foregoing clearly indicates that it is imperative that the Native sons of good families receive adequate educational opportunities. But education should not merely aim at training them for careers as officials; rather it should have a multifarious character, preparing for careers in the sciences, in the arts, or in business ....

Changes are imperative, for it is intolerable that the dominated continue to live as a fish out of water in the midst of a civilization wrought by the alien ruler ....

If the present situation remains unchanged then the Natives, in general, and those of high birth, in particular, may be expected to fade into complete obscurity. This in no way could be in the interest of the Indies. The alien ruler as well as the ruled have a common interest in the intellectual and moral elevation of the dominated.

After this introduction I shall indicate what could be done to encourage Regents to give their sons a better education.

Grade school attendance has nowadays almost become the rule, but one should not expect too much of this education, for as a rule children quit school too early and do not complete the courses successfully. Usually the parents—themselves without the faintest notion of education—consider a knowledge of Dutch more than sufficient, as long as their sons learn a modicum of the spoken and written language .... The Dutch language is, for the Javanese, difficult to master, for their own language has totally different linguistic rules. A few years of study for the Native cannot result in an accurate understanding and knowledge of written and spoken Dutch, especially not if the acquired education is not adequately maintained after he leaves school.

This, however, invariably happens with the Native officials who have completed grade school. They are assigned dull or mechanical work, without being given the opportunity to use their acquired knowledge. Surrounded by his own people a Javanese will remain true to his nature; he has no initiative; energy is unknown to him and thus he returns to his own ways and abandons all he has learned in grade school.

Because all the books on the progress and development in every field are written in Dutch or other foreign languages, a knowledge of any of these tongues is very useful, and should serve him as a tool for the understanding of things that otherwise would remain obscure.

Even though attendance of European schools by Regents' sons may be commonplace, the results in themselves are insignificant, unless one is sure that such training bears fruit. The opportunity to attend the HBS is still only used in exceptional cases, possibly because many do not consider a European education essential.[9]

Therefore, on the whole, training leaves a good deal to be desired for the following reasons.

1. Education is not mandatory and parents do not feel compelled to send their children to school.

The reasons are fatalism and lack of initiative . . . . Certain standards for those who want to succeed must be established. For the Native, fatalistic as he is, will regard requirements imposed upon him as a manifestation of his fate.

2. The Europeans themselves do not agree whether educating the Javanese is advisable.[10]

3. Many parents fear a European education may alienate their children from them, for it may tempt them to become disrespectful toward their superiors or the alien ruler. And nowadays even ordinary Europeans in the interior demand of all Natives faithful compliance with Native forms of respect.

And even though many are aware that the forms of respect are not everywhere the same or equally refined, and not all Natives are familiar with these forms, all Natives are nonetheless treated alike. Innocent candor on the part of a Native, in the eyes of a European, is often considered impertinence. This is why Native officials are nowadays more obsequious than they used to be, for now they vie, as it were, for the observation of the forms of politeness for fear they incur the less pleasant accusation of *"tida taoe adat"* [not knowing custom] . . . .

I believe that the following measures could bring about improvement of the present situation.

1. Provide the prospective official with more opportunities to acquire the desired training and at the same time establish specific requirements for the various positions or duties just as is done for the European . . . .

I proposed this plan to the former Director of Internal Administration . . . in 1871, when as an employee of that Department . . . I was asked to submit a memorandum on this subject. After receiving it, his Honor said, "You live in the clouds; it is easier to submit than to realize such a proposal. . . . "

2. Provide increased opportunities for the training of prospective officials and others by taking the following steps:[11]

a. Enlarge the existing schools for Native officials so that at least 180 students may be placed in each of these schools.

b. Establish a school of the same size in each of the three parts of Java, with each school located in a different town.

c. Require of all prospective administrative officials the same training as the *djaksa* now receives, because the district officials who are the first to investigate all misdemeanors should have the same knowledge of the laws and regulations as the judicial officials.

It would be even more desirable if the Dutch government could create at some stage a separate, well-trained, native judiciary, divorced from the administrative services proper to assist the corps of Dutch judicial officials.

d. Expand the existing school for *doktors djawa,*[12] in the interest of the population, to permit the training of 100 or more candidates. At present the population derives practically no benefit from the *doktors djawa,* because of the limited number of doctors compared with the number of inhabitants leaving the doctors no time to treat the population properly . . . .

e. The school just mentioned is to serve West Java exclusively,[13] a new school with the same enrollment and of the same caliber is to be established in each of the other two provincial capitals.

f. Regulation (d) mentioned also applies to the establishment of schools for midwives.

g. Establish in each of the three provincial capitals a school for the training of *mantris* to be employed by the irrigation service or the Department of Waterworks.

h. Establish, where necessary, similar schools in the Outer Provinces [provinces outside Java].

i. Provide wherever there is a need opportunities for training in all other fields.

Thus the establishment of trade schools is desirable everywhere, especially for the benefit of the lower classes. Presently the Netherlands government is utilizing so few of the abilities with which nature has endowed my fellow countrymen.

j. Demand that all prospective officials pass specific examination requirements for positions of their choice. Among these knowledge of Dutch should be a prerequisite.

k. Require the sons of Regents, in particular, those who are likely to succeed their fathers, to complete either three or five years of high school and, depending on circumstances, to proceed to the higher grades of the school for Native officials.

These rather stringent requirements are imperative because there is a good chance that these young men immediately can be called upon to assume the highest places in our Native administration without first having to occupy lower positions.

l. All the above regulations to become effective, say, ten years from the date of promulgation and to apply only to sons of Native officials who have not yet reached the age of ten at this time.

Those who have met the conditions established for public servants, must, before receiving a permanent assignment, first work for a Regent, Administrative, District, Judicial or Waterworks official, or physician and be entrusted with work commensurate with their training, either in an office or in the field . . . . An apprenticeship of a native *djaksa* under the supervision of administrative officials is deemed indispensable, otherwise the public servant will be ignorant of native institutions, mores, customs and notions and of village life [in general] . . . .

By suggesting these means which may lead to improvements I am not only acting in the interest of my fellow countrymen but also primarily in the interest of the government as well. For it is clearly undesirable that present conditions may inadvertently give rise to others that may nullify all previously made calculations . . . . Good leadership is thus imperative to prevent the emergence of inclinations which are bound to develop from the very nature of the present conditions.

I am ready to relinquish the improvements I have recommended for better ones; my intention was merely to indicate along what lines changes could be made in the interest of the country and the people . . . .

There will now be less crawling. But who cares! In any case the *Hor-*

mat has steadily decreased because of changed conditions. Probably, it will be reduced to a minimum even if nothing is done to change the intellectual development of the Native. Civilized people do know how to comport themselves in society.

Just as Rome was not built in a day, so will the task of civilizing take time. It needs to be accomplished slowly. And gradual change need not instill anguish and fear, certainly not if, as I have suggested, work will start from the top.

The reader of this memorandum should not take offense that the writer has expressed his opinion so frankly. I feel that the Dutchman will all the more appreciate hearing for once the true feelings of the ruled, since he is so rarely given the opportunity to observe the hearts and minds of the brown man. Friends tell one another the truth; enemies hide it from each other. Let us never forget this. By speaking my mind I have acquitted myself of a friend's duty.

NOTES

1. Rulers, in Dutch, *hoofden,* is a somewhat misleading designation, for they were officials appointed by the colonial government, usually, but decreasingly so, from among members of the leading aristocracy. See B. J. O. Schrieke, *Indonesian Sociological Studies* (The Hague: Van Hoeve, 1956), Part I, pp. 188-195.
2. The cultivation system (in Dutch, *cultuur stesel*), a system of forced crop cultivation, was started in 1830 after the devastations of the Java War (1825-1830) necessitated filling the colonial coffers. To ensure the success of the project, the aid of the regents was indispensable. With the virtual abolition of the system by 1870, it actually persisted until 1917 in the West Java Residency of Preangan, the intercession of the aristocracy was no longer sought, and they were gradually bypassed. This was purportedly done in the interest of the indigenous population to protect them from the alleged oppression of their rulers. For arguments favoring direct contact with the population, see Schrieke, *Indonesian Sociological Studies,* p. 194.
3. The Dutch government maintained a consulate in Jidda for the benefit of the Indonesian pilgrims *(hadjis)* to the holy city Mecca. The overwhelming majority of Indonesians are Moslems.
4. The Schools for Native Officials (in Dutch, *hoofdenscholen*) were established in 1878.
5. The Native public schools were established in 1871 and comprised three grades. No Dutch was taught. In 1878 the number of schools (excluding the mission schools) was 354 for the entire archipelago. Widespread dissatisfaction with the results, one-third of the students never completed more than one year of school, led to a reduction of the number of schools and students. See *Verslag van het Inlandsch Onderwijs in Nederlandsch-Indie, 1878-1882* (Batavia: Landsdrukkerij, 1885), p. 46.
6. The schools for Native officials numbered four: three in Java (Bandung, Magelang, and Probolinggo), each with an enrollment of sixty students, and one in Sulawesi (Tondano) with an enrollment of forty. See, *Verslag van het Inlandsch,* Appendix A, p. 269-270.

7. A reorganization of Indonesian grade schools took effect in 1893 when they were divided into first- and second-class schools, the former intended for children of the aristocracy and merchants, the latter—far more limited in scope—for those of the lower classes. See *Publicaties Hollandsch-Inlandsche Onderwijs Commissie* (Weltevreden: Landsdrukkerij, 1930) 9, part 2, p. 15.

8. Hadiningrat here refers to the custom among the Javanese to address each other according to rank, status, and class, so-called low Javanese *(Djawa ngoko)* or high Javanese *(Djawa kromo)*. For a description of the relationship between European and indigenous administration, see Een Regent "Nota betreffende de verhouding tusschen het Europeesch en het inlandsch bestuur op Java en Madoera," *De Indische Gids,* 1889, vol. 2, pp. 1521-1524.

9. *HBS,* H(ogere) B(urger) S(chool), high school. There were three such schools in Java at that time. Since 1874 Indonesians were admitted to the schools. In 1898/99 fourteen Indonesians were enrolled. See *Algemeen Verslag van de Staat van het Middelbaar en Lager Onderwijs voor Europeanen 1898-99* (Batavia: Landsdrukkerij, 1900), p. 14.

10. Hadiningrat's observation was correct. Ever since the Dutch inaugurated an educational policy in the mid-nineteenth century many articles had appeared questioning the desirability of "elevating," the colonized. Throughout the nineteenth century, Dutch educational policy was basically utilitarian. See Greta Wilson, "Dutch Educational Policy in Indonesia 1850-1900," *Asian Profile* 3, no. 1 (February, 1975): 70-72.

11. In 1900 the *hoofdenscholen* were reorganized and renamed OSVIA (Opleidingsschool voor Inlandsche Ambtenaren, Training school for Native Officials). The schools trained *djaksa* as well as officials. Attendance was made mandatory; a knowledge of Dutch and previous attendance of a European grade school became a prerequisite. See, J. Habbema, "Hollandsch voor aanstaande inlandsche ambtenaren en onderwijzers," *De Indische Gids* 2 (1901) p. 840. Habbema was a member of the commission recommending reorganization.

12. The *School voor Doktor Djawa* (school for Javanese physicians) was established in 1851 in Batavia. The original plan had been to set up several schools in various parts of the country. The Batavia school, as its name indicated, was originally only intended for Java. *Ontwikkeling van het Geneeskundig Onderwijs in Weltevreden 1851-1926* (Weltevreden: Kolff, 1926), p. 4.

13. Java was administratively divided into three parts: West, Central, and East Java.

P. A. Achmad Djajadiningrat

P. A. Achmad Djajadiningrat:
A Westernized Aristocrat
(1877-1943)

Achmad Djajadiningrat, scion of an old Banten family became the first regent to receive a formal western education. An account of his experiences, published in 1936 as his *Memoirs*,[1] makes very entertaining reading and provides an excellent depiction of colonial society.

He was born in Kabajan Banten on August 16, 1877. Islamic training came first; the teacher made him aware that he, the son of an official who worked for the *kafir* (unbeliever), was somehow tainted too, and he was subjected to frequent snides.[2] Then followed western education of a sort: Dutch tutors succeeded one another rapidly.[3]

On the advice and under the tutelage of the Advisor for Native Affairs C. Snouck Hurgronje, Achmad went to Batavia. He enrolled in a private Dutch school, but because his illustrious name was feared to be offensive to some parents, the principal had a solution: Achmad became William of Banten and his grade-school days proceeded without incident.[4]

Upon completion of grade school, Achmad enrolled in the Dutch high school and soon experienced that not only society, but the law too discriminated against the natives. Engaging in pranks with some Dutch friends resulted in a mere admonition for the latter and had Achmad not been a regent's son, his name would have been entered for posterity in the police records.[5]

Upon graduation Achmad joined the native administration and quickly advanced through the ranks. From 1901 until 1924 he was Regent of Serang, and was from there transferred to the Batavia regency. In addition to his work as regent, he also served the colonial government and was a member of eleven commissions dealing with such divers subjects as declining prosperity, administrative reforms, and improved education.[6] By virtue of his position he was chairman of his regency council, and served as a member of the provincial council of West Java, and from 1918 until 1930, of the People's Council. When the Council of the Indies, the advisory body to the governor-general, was enlarged from four to six members, Djajadiningrat was one of the two Indonesians appointed in 1930. Because of ill health he resigned from the government in 1936.

While a member of the People's Council, Djajadiningrat was affiliated with the Netherlands Indies Liberal League, a political party seeking Indonesian autonomy and advocating equal protection under the law for the various ethnic groups in the archipelago.[7] When, however, abolition of the penal code was discussed in the People's Council, Djajadiningrat voted with the majority to retain it.[8]

Djajadiningrat was a benevolent paternalist, well aware of the racial and social intricacies of his colonial society. He professed to have sympathy for the nationalist movement but had no use for demagogues. Like Hadiningrat he believed that the prestige of the old aristocracy could be restored, if members of this group were willing to make adjustments.

An intelligent and proud man, Djajadiningrat must have found colonialism obnoxious and humiliating for the inlander, but even more so for the native rulers. His memoirs are replete with instances of slights incurred and not just those inflicted by members of Dutch officialdom. Thus he relates an incident which occurred in 1902 while dining in a Surabaya hotel. He overheard two ill-mannered young Dutchmen remarking of him: "What kind of an ape is that?" "Look, look, he eats with fork and spoon!" "Gosh, he drinks wine!" "By Jove, he even understands Dutch!" A Dutch official who also overheard the conversation apologized to Djajadiningrat, who professed not to be vexed by the incident. That he spelled it out in detail speaks volumes.[9]

Djajadiningrat can best be described as a transition figure. His heritage made him part of the old corps of officials, but his western education and his keen perception of colonial society made him realize that the nationalist movement was proceeding without the regents and, in fact, had turned against them. He was a reformer, but only sought changes for a society that would put him and his ilk in the driver's seat.

NOTES

1. *Herinneringen van Pangeran Ario Achmad Djajadiningrat* (Batavia: Kolff, 1936).
2. *Ibid.,* pp. 20–23.
3. *Ibid.,* pp. 26–28, 31–33.

4. *Ibid.*, pp. 67-68.
5. *Ibid.*, pp. 78-79.
6. *Ibid.*, pp. 316-317.
7. *Volksraadboekje 1927-28,* 3d. ed. (Weltevreden: Kolff 1928), pp. 84-85.
8. H. G. Heijting, *De Koelie Wetgeving* (The Hague: van Stockum, 1925), pp. 151-152.
9. Djajadiningrat, *Herinneringen,* pp. 241-242.

Editor's Introduction:
Development and Demise of the Sarekat Islam

The Sarekat Islam, established in 1912, had developed out of the Sarekat Dagang Islam, a trading organization aimed at curbing the encroachment of the Chinese merchants on the Javanese batik industry.

Under the leadership of H. O. S. Tjokroaminoto, the Sarekat Islam grew swiftly and saw its membership increase to around half a million by 1917. The party's program called for the promotion of a commercial spirit among the Indonesian people and the advancement of their spiritual and material interests, thus contributing to their elevation; the promotion of religious life according to Islamic tenets; and the opposition against erroneous concepts on Islam.

When communists infiltrated the Sarekat Islam some of the leaders were instrumental in forcing adoption of party discipline. This brought about a showdown with the communists but also heralded the demise of the party.

In 1923 the party was reorganized and renamed Partij Sarekat Islam and its religious basis emphasized. The total number of members remained small throughout its existence.

The Sarekat Islam[1]

THE NATIVE ADMINISTRATION AND THE MOHAMMEDAN CLERGY TOWARD THE SAREKAT ISLAM.

The native administrators with an education and point of view comparable to mine regarded the birth of the Sarekat Islam (S.I.) as an occasion for rejoicing. They saw it as a manifestation of the people's consciousness arousing high expectations which in turn promoted efforts to realize these expectations. To the older more conservative officials the Sarekat Islam seemed like a nightmare. At the time, I sought the opinion of my district heads about the Sarekat Islam.

One of them, a regent's son who had received an old-fashioned upbringing wrote:

> Every native administrator who expresses his opinion honestly will never wish the Sarekat Islam well. For every human being enjoys seeing others defer to him and act as a slave. It appears now certain that the Sarekat Islam will put an end to this. Besides the Sarekat Islam will in time find a response among the people and many administrators fear that the native official will be ousted from its traditional position.

There was another group in Banten which did not favorably regard the Sarekat Islam, namely, the religious teachers and Moslem scribes. As Assistant *Wedana,* I had discovered that the majority of these men performed their task primarily for a living; religious considerations usually were of minor importance. As long as they, in their opinion, enjoy rights and fair treatment, they remain law-abiding citizens and I would not like to wish them any changes in their day-to-day life, which is without exception far from unpleasant. They are conservative and attempt to suppress any innovation which could bring about changes, in whatever field, in the existing conditions which they consider a danger to their material interest....

A saying of the Prophet, usually cited just before the reading or the discussion of the holy text, is used by them as a weapon. This is:

> Beware of new things, for every new thing is heresy; all heresy is error; and all error belongs in the fire of hell.

It stands to reason that if the religious teachers' influence is great, their action is a not-to-be underestimated impediment for the normal development of their country and people.

If, however, they are honest and dispassionate, then in the interest of peace, they would not have any objections to losing part of their material advantages or status, and little opposition needs to be feared from them. The religious leaders can sometimes exert a beneficial influence in cases where a person may act rashly and expediently, especially at the present time. These days, in particular, when political ideas are advanced that advocate bringing about the country's independence as soon as possible, one often hears recited for the masses from the holy scriptures:

> A kingdom may survive without belief, but not without justice.

Thus the religious teachers who in the past have obstructed the native officials with religious arguments, by the execution of new measures of the government, have become, as far as the Sarekat Islam is concerned, the friends of these officials, using the same weapons with which they formerly opposed them.

From the Dutch point of view the Sarekat Islam in Banten was and remained a danger because the religious element played an important role in the movement.

DEVELOPMENT OF THE SAREKAT ISLAM IN BANTEN

Raden Gunawan was the first advocate of the Sarekat Islam who came to Banten with instructions from the Central Committee to establish a branch in Serang; he discussed the plan with me. I had no objection but stipulated that the head of the branch preferably should be a man with western education. I recommended my brother Hasan, who had graduated from the HBS (five-year curriculum) and who for health reasons had not become an official.

I had discussed this matter beforehand with the Advisor for Native Affairs who concurred with my idea. Thus my brother Hasan became president of the Sarekat Islam branch in Banten. With application and dedication he tried to make his organization flourish and make it serve the interest of the country and people. Soon the organization had its own weekly publication, *Mimbar,* meaning pulpit.

In addition, the organization established a commercial enterprise called Pirukan Pribumi. They also operated a cooperative store. It stands to reason that the Sarekat Islam publication in Serang sometimes criticized administration and government. Curiously the public could not make the distinction between spiritual and blood brothers.

There were people who believed that the strictures were mine and that I used the Sarekat Islam as a sounding board. Naturally my brother Hasan had freedom of action. It would have been unfair toward the organization for me to try and influence his actions.

The Sarekat Islam exerted an irresistible magnetism on the young native intellectuals, those who had been trained for the native administration.[2] Many of them became members and thus many qualified men were lost to native officialdom. The government, although alerted to this by qualified men, did not bring about any changes. The position of the native official remained poor, both financially and spiritually. Their starting salary was still fifteen guilders a month. Concerning the psychological aspect of the position, a remarkable article had appeared by the *controleur B. B. J. J.* van Helsdingen. From this I would like to cite only three points.

1. The lack of binding uniform rules on appointments or promotions (ranklists are of limited usefulness for they are not adhered to by the residents).

2. The lack of supervision by the interested parties and public opinion.

3. The existing system of recruiting native officials by hiring members of the same family and the absence of a separate corps of native officials.

... Nonetheless the native administration was not despised not even by the men of the Sarekat Islam. The best-educated men of the Sarekat Islam, in general, were not sparse in their criticism of the actions of the government and the administration. If any of them exceeded the limit of acceptability, then the Advisor of Native Affairs stepped in, warningly raising his finger, saying: "Watch out, little fellow, you are going too far!" Whereupon the culprit invariably replied:

> I cannot act otherwise, for if I do, the Sarekat Islam does not want me any longer as a member. And then what can I do for a living?

On the question subsequently posed if he would be willing to return to the native administration, the eager reply was: "Yes, thank you very much sir!" But securing such a Sarekat Islam man a position in the native administration was easier said than done. No administrator would be willing to have such a man among his workers.

It is rather interesting to hear how such a person was treated by the Advisor of Native Affairs. He was asked to express his loyalty and adherence toward Dutch authority in an article of a widely read Dutch newspaper, so that the attention of the regional administration was assured. Subsequently a resident had to be found who, as far as *hormat* [usage] was concerned, was *plus royaliste que le roi*. For a Sarekat Islam man could no longer walk without shoes and could no longer make a *sembah*. This he had to learn anew. . . .

POOR CONTINUED DEVELOPMENT OF THE SAREKAT ISLAM

Apparently the time was not ripe for the existence of a body that, next to or above the administration, could provide leadership to the population. Even the Sarekat Islam did not succeed to dispute that leadership. Because the time was not propitious the Sarekat Islam could not grow and develop as was originally expected, notwithstanding the continued accommodating attitude of the government.

In the beginning the Sarekat Islam was not a political party; its attitude toward the government was very submissive. It declared everywhere that it would strive for the elevation of the people of the Indies, in cooperation with the government, without violating the laws. The aim was only to point out less desirable conditions and leave the ways of improvement to the government. But when the movement "The Indies Ready for Defense" started and the Sarekat Islam had to determine its attitude toward this movement, it became clear that the Sarekat Islam was also a political organization whose goal was independence of the Indies. Then the leadership lost control, until the plot of the secret Sarekat Islam Section-B was discovered in West Java, and this spelled the end of the Sarekat Islam's existence.[3]

NOTES

1. *Herinneringen van Pangeran Ario Achmad Djajadiningrat* (Amsterdam and Batavia: G. Kolff, 1936), pp. 285-289.
2. The lack of interest among the young aristocracy for positions in the native administration was a source of concern to the colonial government. Several graduates of the training schools for native officials, became prominent in the nationalist movement, one of them was H. O. S. Tjokroaminoto, a leader of the Sarekat Islam.
3. B-1 Affair, also known as Garut Affair, concerned a religious leader who refused to pay taxes and was said to have plotted against the government (1919).

Editor's Introduction:
Regency Councils

Changes in the structure of the native administration were inaugurated with the establishment of regency councils between 1920 and 1926. This went hand in hand with other changes: the emancipation of some of the regents (in Dutch, *ontvoogding*), the abolition of the position of *controleur* (the lowest rank in the Dutch administrative hierarchy), and the assumption of the duties of the *controleur* by the regent. Several regencies were combined.

Although, when the changes were conceived in the early decades of the twentieth century, fundamental changes were indeed envisaged, by the time they were implemented, colonial policy had veered away from its liberal course.

Thus the measures taken were halfhearted. Only a few of the regents (Djajadiningrat was one) were emancipated, and the position of the *controleur* was restored in the nineteen thirties.

The Position of the Regents on Java and Madura in the Present Administrative System[1]

Mr. Chairman! No position regulated by Indies law has set in motion—and still does—so many tongues and pens, has experienced so many phases of development, or rather of dismantling or perhaps metamorphosis, as that of the regent of Java and Madura. To date several statesmen and scholars disagree on what the function of the regent should be.

To examine the present position of the regency and its future, it is rather important to consider the evolution of this position and its changes.

When consulting the Javanese chronicles and the Chinese and European travel accounts, one will notice that the Hindu-Javanese empire had reached its pinnacle of splendor in the first half of the fourteenth century. It extended not only over Java, but well-nigh over the whole East Indian archipelago and Malaya. Politically the country was divided into a heartland, which was directly administered by the monarch, and feudal fiefs, headed by dignitaries who possessed a great deal of autonomy. As a result each one was, in his own territory, no less powerful than the king himself, so that in the eyes of their subjects they occupied the same position as the actual sovereign.

The old Javanese epic Negarakrtagama teaches us, among other things, with what splendor and pomp these vassals appeared, even in the capital of the realm.

In fact there were many among these vassals who, primarily through economic revival in their regions, became increasingly confident and finally tried to secure independence from the feudal lord. A protracted struggle ensued between the heartland and the vassal states, ending with the complete annihilation of the power of the vassals concomitant with the total exhaustion of the realm of Java, which was barely able to stand its ground.

Many of these small vassal states came within the power orbit of the East India Company, which tried to restore order by appointing an indigenous administration headed by rulers called "regents."

The first regents of the East India Company were not equal in power and prestige; some were in charge of large areas and were descendants of old Mataram vassals. On the other hand, others whose birth was taken into little consideration, had little power. They were more or less under the influence of the former, whom the company particularly tried to uphold before the population by letting them retain their former rights as much as possible. Thus their subjects considered them as [they had] their former *bupati* or monarch, although they were actually regular officials appointed, promoted, dismissed, and penalized.

They had, among other powers, the authority to appoint and dismiss all officials and lower officials within their region. With these officials, consisting primarily of their relatives, they conducted their administration without virtually any control. Moreover, they were outwardly treated more as vassals than as officials. The right of their heirs to succeed them was invariably assured.

Although this system left much to be desired, particularly as far as the common man was concerned, it was in any case a continuation of old customs, so that chiefs and population still formed a harmonious unity.

Perhaps consistent implementation and development along those lines would have been a blessing for Java. But alas, the company only adhered to it with ulterior motives [in mind]. They departed from the premise: The Javanese would prefer to be skinned, and rightly so, by their own kind, than be bothered by foreigners.

At the time the population could indeed accept a great deal from its chiefs. However, they inevitably discovered in whose interest they were "skinned."

I refrain from enumerating a number of other measures the company took concerning the native administration, actions which turned out to be disastrous for the position of the regent. I merely wish to point out that, already at the time of the East India Company, the regent, in the eyes of the population, was only an instrument of a foreign power.

That does not alter the fact that there were still regents who, because of their personality, birth, or the manner in which they acted in the interest of the population under their care, still exerted a great deal of influence. . . .[2]

These were the conditions under which the defunct goods and chattels of the East India Company were accepted by the Netherlands commonwealth. At the time there blew a strong democratic wind in Europe which spread to the colonies. In the beginning one would have wanted to introduce a democratic regime here too, but soon would have realized that the population was still too uneducated and had been subjugated for too long under an autocratic administration to accept democracy successfully.

However, it was considered necessary to review thoroughly the administrative system in the Indies, which was soon implemented. The result, among others, was that the regents became regular officials, who no longer had the authority to appoint and dismiss officials and were even required to carry out orders of the European officeholders supervising them. For the first time they were given extensive instructions. From then on the regents' power was continuously curtailed.

The European administration had to make direct contact with the indigenous population, preferably excluding the regents. To what extent the regents were pushed into the background can be deduced from the words of G. G. van der Capellen:

> Nearly everywhere the regents were treated with contempt and barred from participation in the administration; and among the European officials the idea prevailed that the regents could be designated as superfluous parts in the administration.

Finally the feelings were such that abolition of the position of regents was considered. This was quite understandable; for a profoundly democratic-thinking people as the Dutch, the deeds and actions of the regents of those days toward the population were too autocratic. Protection of the indigenous people from extortion by their chiefs became an item on the agenda of the European administration.

The regent's ancestry was no longer considered: adventurers, a former cook of a resident, even a former slave or serf have occupied the high position. Nonetheless their influence on the population was not completely lost, especially not of those regents who were descendants of the old administrative or ruling families. The number of those, fortunately, was still rather large. Their knowledge of the country and the people remained outstanding, primarily attributable to their way of life.

Meanwhile the Java War broke out, and the regents, in the areas ravaged by war, rendered excellent services to the Netherlands government. Some years later the so-called cultivation system was introduced in Java, and to ensure its success, the authority of the regents was deemed indispensable. At that time the feeling among those in power, in the Netherlands as well as in the Indies, had mellowed.

No one any longer believed:

> ... to win over the population ... by protecting them against their chiefs, by countering the so-called extortions and to cultivate ... a feeling of independence. ...

Commissioner General J. van den Bosch continued:

> Thus we must try ... in every acceptable way to obligate the Chiefs to us and I have tried to do so by respecting their rights as much as possible, by treating them with deference and even with friendliness ... and finally to treat them in such a way that they have reason to be happier under our administration than under their own monarchs.

This basic principle was finally incorporated and the rights and duties of the regents were regulated by law stating that the regent as such is at the helm of the native population of the regency where he is appointed, responsible for the preservation of order in his resort and, in general, will act in the interest of the people.

It is obvious what an important and responsible position the regent had. And besides his task was often difficult to perform. Under the rules he was not only the head of the population, but an official as well, and as such he had to obey the orders of his European supervisor. But what to do when these were, in his opinion, at variance with the interests of the population or would lead to disturbing peace and order? At the time those regents who completely understood and tried to execute their tasks were referred to as troublemakers.

But the cultivation system was discarded and the Java War forgotten. Again the European administration tried to communicate directly with the native population, excluding the regents. The rationale was that the regents, because of the low level of their general education, were unable to satisfy ever-increasing requirements so that not without harm could an "immediate leadership" over the population be consigned to them.

The problem of the level of general education was also acknowledged by the indigenous populace. I shall discuss this later.

The improved training of native officials, which started in 1879 [1878] was reaping benefits, but it proved to be too low in view of the prevailing conditions. Even the graduates of the so-called schools for chiefs were considered unqualified by the European administration to assume, independently, immediate leadership over the native population.

In those days there were some regents, whose general level of education was not at all lower than that of the European administrators and who orally and in writing tried to assert all their legal rights and duties as regents, but they were just mavericks, and their cries were often lost.

In official circles the opinion prevailed that as long as the immediate leadership remained unenforced, many of the government's or administration's measures concerning the indigenous population could not be guaranteed lasting success.

Some Netherlanders, who eminently knew and understood the Indonesian people,[3] pleaded forcefully and skillfully for the gradual "emancipation" of the Indonesian administration on Java and Madura. They did not wish to see emancipation introduced everywhere immediately. Only in those places where the native administration and the regent, in particular, were considered capable of handling the new responsibilities. The intention was to transfer the responsibilities of the assistant resident, as head of the local administration, to the regent.

The pressure on the government to institute reforms was only reluctantly complied with. The native administration was tentatively emancipated in only one regency, but not as was planned originally: only some insignificant administrative powers of the assistant resident and the *controleur* were transferred to the regent and the district head. The European administration remained intact, so that the big word "emancipation" was, in fact, unable to accomplish any change in the existing conditions.

Meanwhile Dutch statesmen had not abandoned the idea to steer the administration of the Netherlands Indies into more democratic channels. The new direction of colonial policy yielded, especially in the field of education, important results while the task of the government became increasingly complex and differentiated.

Whereas in the first half of the nineteenth century, Commissioner van den Bosch did not wish to see that the indigenous population "became imbued with the spirit of independence from its chiefs (appointed or recognized by the Government)," in the beginning of the twentieth century this spirit expressed itself of its own accord and expanded quickly. New, more modern political movements, completely independent of the administration, emerged among the population, which especially rebelled against the autocratic character of the existing administrative system. That the native administration, in particular, became the target of criticism was not surprising; for in many instances they were still a buffer between the authorities and the population. Obviously the inner respect of the population for the regents was not considerably undermined.

Yet there were regents who, cognizant of changed times, tried to lead this movement in the right direction. As a rule, however, they could not secure support from their European supervisors, and some of the leaders were . . . described as politically unreliable.

However, it was finally realized that the administrative policy in the

Indies needed to be changed. Skipping the enactment of the so-called decentralization legislation and the establishment of the People's Council, which were relatively insignificant for the position of the regent, I shall speak of the so-called administrative reforms which indeed brought considerable changes in the relationship of the regent and the population, on one hand, and the European administration, on the other hand.

Article 121 of the Act on the Governance of the Netherlands Indies provided for the establishment of part of the provinces as autonomous communities. It is primarily the implementation of this legal provision that brought about an important change in the position of the regents, to wit, the institution of regency councils . . . the council shall consist of members drawn from among the indigenous non-Netherlands subjects, Netherlands subjects and non-Netherlands foreign subjects . . . the indigenous are recruited partly by election, partly by appointment . . . and shall constitute a majority in the council.

The principal powers of the regency council are: to regulate and administer the affairs of the regency, to represent the interests of the regency and its inhabitants before the governor-general, the People's Council, the Provincial Council as well as the Council of Delegates, the governor and the resident; to negotiate loans, levy taxes, and establish regulations. From among its membership the regency council may elect delegates.

This assembly of delegates is primarily entrusted with the execution of decisions of the regency council; cooperation in the execution of national and provincial regulations (this cooperation is not expressly required of other bodies or officials); care for the adequate preparation of all those matters which must be given to the council to consider and resolve. Theoretically the rights and duties of the regency council can be considered important.

What is the function of the regent with regard to this council? In the first place, he is the chairman of the council, and as such he is entrusted with the execution of the decisions of the council and of the council of delegates. He is also the chairman of the latter body. However, he is empowered to vote against the implementation of decisions which, in his opinion, violate national or provincial regulations or the general interest.

Finally the administration of the regency consists of: the regency council, the assembly of delegates—wherever this exists, and the regent.

Thus in every regency whereto administrative reform was implemented, one finds a body, where even simple *desa* people may belong, governing and cogoverning next to and even without the regent . . . which can represent the interests of the area at higher levels.

I say next to the regent, for he finds in his new instructions (Gouvernements besluit May 8, 1926), a provision that he still, to the best of his abilities [,] looks after the interests of the regency of which he is the administrator and promotes the prosperity of the native population, over which he has the immediate leadership. (Article 10.)

He is the administrator of a body, wherein simple *desa* people and even recalcitrant nationalist leaders may occupy seats. He is exposed to public criticism of such people! One wonders if this does not severely undermine the authority of the regent.

Particularly those who believe that on Java the glory of the umbrella can still be restored see in this the commencement of the destruction of the native administration the pillars of Dutch authority.[4] They therefore wish to undo the changes, so that the regent may be tucked away again in the *pusaka* case, the case of holy objects. Thus he at least will have nothing more to do openly with the regency council, and the daily leadership of that body will be consigned to a *patih,* one below him in rank, or to another person.

I hope the government will never yield to such an instigation, for it is my firm conviction that this will lead to a complete elimination of the regents' authority over the native population. One should not forget that the Javanese of today has changed. Regardless of the ruler, he will no longer expect an invisible *berkah* or blessing, which could be secured by burning a *menjam* in his regent's honor. He wants to see action. The regent should be provided with opportunities to show by his deeds that he loves his land and people. Under the present circumstances, this is the only way to strengthen the authority of the regent, and the existence of the regency council gives this chance.

Ladies and gentlemen, undoubtedly one expects to hear from me not theoretical observations, but practical experiences. For more than a year and a half I was president of the regency council in Batavia, which certainly is not the easiest in West Java; for among its members are politically trained Indonesians, *desa* people who previously have never been under the authority of a regent, some intellectuals, an engineer, a lawyer, a medical doctor, and someone who studied at the commercial college in Rotterdam. Yet, I can declare that, as far as my official work is concerned, this period was the best of my thirty years of administrative experience. On my own initiative, in the interest of my region, I could implement rules, albeit of little significance because of the limited powers and the poor financial position of the council that I was in charge of. My advice on the needs and requirements of the population in my regency was no longer stifled; whatever the result was, my voice always was heard by the public, by the administrators, and by the government. I was in charge of certain matters, and I felt that finally a way and an opportunity were opened to me as regent to secure gradually the "immediate leadership" of the indigenous population under my jurisdiction.

This statement, which I have reiterated, has been countered with:

Naturally, you have some political schooling behind you and have thus acquired a political opinion which is perhaps quite susceptible to [accepting] institutions such as the regency councils. Besides you have received an education different from that of most of the regents, who never have participated in politics, have grown up in a completely autocratic administrative system, have at most a diploma from a training school for native officials.

There were regents who, before the new institution came into effect, shied away from their new task. But it was apparently a fear of the unknown. Moreover, the provisions—especially the administrative regulations pertaining to the regency council—are so very complicated and voluminous that it must have caused shivers to those entrusted with its execution.

But as far as I know in the areas where the administrative reforms have been effective for some years, there is not one regent, who finds his work too heavy or disagreeable; on the contrary, some of them are, albeit silently, enthusiastic about it.

Why is the establishment of the regency council for the regent so encouraging? . . .

According to instructions, the regent is committed to advance the prosperity of his regency. Naturally he is very familiar with the needs and requirements of the population, and as a rule he knows generally how these can be satisfied. But prosperity is a broad and elastic concept. Hygiene, modern technique, economics, constitutional and administrative law all can contribute to this [prosperity]. The regent does not and cannot know everything, often he will not be able to realize his ideas or present these as acceptable proposals. However he can transmit these ideas to the assembly of delegates, where he will find experts in many fields. There he will find technicians, lawyers, medical doctors, and industrialists who are not his superiors but his peers. Among them he can express himself freely. Under his leadership in that assembly a certain idea can be concretized, and its soundness tested by the opinion of the representatives of the population, the regency council.

Obviously, the regent, with confidence, can implement a matter already accepted by the council. In this implementation he is completely free; he may act according to his own views.

With these examples I believe I have indicated sufficiently the kind of freshness brought about in the work of the regents by the establishment of the regency council. Yet there are dangers, which can kill the initiative of the regent as president of the council.

One of these is Article 124 of the regency council ordinance, which stipulates that the regent is charged with the supervision of the regency council. For there are still residents who, purportedly to prevent unpleasant conflicts, exert gentle pressure on the regent not to submit proposals to the regency council or assembly of delegates, unless these proposals have been thoroughly discussed with them [the residents]. In view of the existing relationships this might hamper the regent and could have a paralyzing effect on his activities, aside from the possibility that he will become a mouthpiece of the European administration.

I wonder whether such supervision is necessary, whether sufficient compliance is not ensured by Article 25 of the regency ordinance which provides that the regent has the power to disregard decisions of the regency council that are in his opinion violative of national or provincial regulations or the national interest and to notify the regency council, the assembly of delegates and the assembly of deputies of his objections?

The second danger lies in the general educational level of the regents. To effectively lead a body that might consist of university-trained members, one should have attained an educational standard higher than that of a primary or secondary school. Not only in the regency council, but especially in the assembly of delegates, the regent should be capable of asserting himself, if he does not want to lose actual leadership.

So far as the education of the native officials is concerned the government generally lags behind. Already in the beginning of the nineteenth century, Baud complained that the sons of native chiefs in the Indies did not have the opportunity to obtain the education indispensable for becoming a native official.[5] In 1845 he urged the Indies government to establish educational institutions in Java for the sons of Javanese chiefs. The first *hoofdenschool* was established only in 1879 [sic 1878].[6] However, as I have briefly indicated, its results were considered inadequate because of the ever increasing demands on the administration.

In 1893 the well-known, late Regent of Demak proposed to upgrade this training. But to this the director of Binnenlandsch Bestur (Dutch civil administration) replied: "You are living in the clouds." Twenty years later a government commission was established in the Indies for the reorganization of the so-called Training Schools for Native Officials. One of the commission members was a regent who urged the substantial improvement of the level of the preparatory education. He, too, received the reply from the chairman of the commission, who happened to be the director of Binnenlandsch Bestur. "Naturally you would prefer that the prospective native administrative officials receive a university training." "Yes," continued the regent, "if that is at all possible, for in about a decade the demands on the administration will be so extensive that even the training proposed by me will be insufficient." The regent subsequently introduced a minority report on the matter. But this new training will undoubtedly no longer be sufficient for the regent in view of his new function. As a matter of fact this has been fully recognized by the present officeholders.

In 1927 the Regents Association, Sedyo Mulyo, convened in Batavia, where the training of prospective regents was discussed. Present were thirty-seven regents who declared unanimously that university training, at least equal to that of European administrative officials, should be required.

Does the government still doubt the need for better education? Or are there possibly other, for instance, financial, reasons? But could not this training—without excessive high costs—take place at the existing Law School in Batavia?

The regent is not only president of the regency council and executor of the decisions of that body, he also has to fulfill, in part, his former administrative function, which rests on autocratic foundations. In this, too, an important change has taken place. According to his new instructions the regent is no longer the head of his population, but only of the native administration in his regency. He is thus no longer considered head of the people but is an ordinary official. Besides he is no longer responsible for the preservation of law and order in his regency, although he is still in charge of it. This is probably because he does not have the necessary means at his disposal; the government still refuses to bring the only modern-equipped police force in the Indies, the field police, directly under the jurisdiction of the regents.

Occasionally the regent has difficulties in the execution of his new ruling task because of his relationship with the assistant resident.

In former days, the European administrative official, the *controleur*, followed the regent in the execution of his task like a shadow. Now his position, primarily of an economic, social, and administrative nature, is completely absorbed into the native administration.

Therefore the present assistant resident, who took the place of the *controleur*, has in this area little left to do. Yet it is considered necessary that the young assistant resident, in particular, in the interest of acquiring practical education performs the work of the former *controleur*. There are residents who, contrary to the intention of the lawmaker, place them [the assistant residents] in that position [of the former *controleur*]. This sometimes leads to conflict with the regent.

I wonder if it would not be possible to have these young European administrative officials work for the regents, providing them with an opportunity to acquire a knowledge of the practical operation of native administration in general. Thus, they will become well-versed in everything pertaining to the function of the regent and the regency council.

Summing up, I shall conclude with the question "Has the status of the regent in the administrative system declined?" Theoretically, this seems true. From leader of the population he has been downgraded to a common official; from a responsible maintainer of authority to a simple adviser; his words and deeds are subject, in public, to criticism from even the simple *desa* people, even of revolutionary nationalist leaders; and he is no longer free in the promotion of the prosperity of the population. I say theoretically, for as you have observed from my arguments, in practice there lies in that system a hopeful future for the native administration in general and the regent in particular. And that future rests with the regency council: the more this body gains in power and strength, the stronger the native administration will become.

One cannot imagine a more democratic institution than a municipality in the Netherlands. I have visited a municipality there, headed by a mayor who has served for more than thirty years. With pride he pointed out the many improvements brought about during his administration. On one occasion I mingled with the burghers. One of them said proudly pointing to the burgomaster, "There is the father of our citizens."

Could not the regent, too, along democratic channels, become the father of the population of his regency?[7]

I see the focal point of the work of the regent in the realm of the regency council, the regent as chairman of the assembly of delegates.[8] In this body of competent men the regent has the opportunity to develop his ideas on administrative matters and express them in proposals. When he brings the proposal to the council, he has the chance to exchange views again with the council. What will happen when this is delegated to someone else? Then the regent does not participate in the discussion and is unfamiliar with the proposal. If the chairman of the regency council, for instance, would be the *patih,* one might assume that the regent does not know anything about it! He will have no part in the execution of the matter discussed in the regency council. The *patih* would, more or less, even have to give orders. The regent would be completely outside all this. However, if the regent is the chairman then he will be the first to prepare matters, subsequently defend them in the council, and finally implement them.

In every area the regent has the opportunity to take the initiative in making proposals to the regency council: the construction of roads; the building of markets; the implementation of projects of the central authorities; and he has the chance to ensure benefits for his regency, thus enhancing his status. I recall that during my regency there existed a small market that had a very good future, with favorable prospects because of the hinterland, but its development was hampered because it lacked an effective connection with the main road. As a result of the efforts of the regent, who proposed a subsidy in the regency council, the linkage was secured. This small act was felt throughout the whole regency. If one leaves the initiative to someone other than the regent, then all improvements will be to the other's benefit and not to the regent's.

As for emancipation . . . I myself was emancipated, and this gave me the right to appoint policemen at a salary of fifteen guilders a month, to issue licenses in some agrarian matters, as well as some other prerogatives of such minor significance that I no longer remember them. Thus the emancipation did not amount to much. What I have emphasized in particular is that, under emancipation, the relationship between the regent, on the one hand, and the assistant resident and the *controleur,* on the other, has not changed. Originally the intention was to eliminate somewhat the European administrative official, but, in fact, this never occurred, the position remained intact, and the relationship between the regent and *BB* was unaffected.

I concede that, as a result of the emancipation, the status of the native administration has been elevated a bit. The population has felt this in the investigation of *desa* complaints, which now can be done by the district heads. But actual conditions have not changed.

Mr. Bergemeier quoted from Mr. Schrieke's book, which I regret I have not had the occasion to read during my busy leave. However, I do not agree that the electoral system can incite the population. There is a commission for the preparation of elections, which consists of the district head, subdistrict head, and the *penghulu.*

This commission goes to the electoral district and calls the voters together. Then they ask: how many candidates do you have? The reply is: this one and that one, and so forth. Take, for instance, five candidates. They are placed in a row. The commission will now ask: who wants Mr. A for an elector? The voters who want him, sit behind him. The same takes place with subsequent candidates, B and so on. Whoever has the most voters behind him gets the most votes and becomes elector. How can in such an amiable election uprising take place? When the electors are chosen they go to the capital city and fill out an election ballot. The voting is secret. I see no possibility of sedition here.

Naturally party alignment cannot be altogether avoided. Meanwhile I have observed that in the second election for the regency council more officials were elected. This is the result of noncooperation. I would have considered it quite useful if some communists would have entered the regency council. I would have considered this a safety valve. Naturally the regent must be able to deal with them. Already he has the advantage that he stands far above them in knowledge of procedures. This strengthens him considerably. In the general discussion in the regency council anything may be brought up by the members. Therefore, how the regent himself acts is important. Once when in the regency council in Batavia, a member complained that everything only leads to tax increase and another disagreed, I simply referred the first speaker to the arguments of the second speaker.

The people who are elected to the regency are quite considerate. I recall a meeting where a few members complained bitterly about the operation of the credit system in Batavia. I advised the complainants that after the agenda they would have the opportunity to voice their objections, which, if necessary, I would convey to the authorities. It was a long meeting that continued into the night; at the end of it I wanted to give these members a chance to voice their complaint; but they had reconsidered, saying, "Mr. Regent already looks so tired!"

Besides the regent is always the leader of the regency council. He would not want to make a distinction between the regent and the council; both must grow together. One should take into account that the regency councils have been in operation for only a few years, however, their significance has not been realized everywhere. The population should be aware that a council of trustworthy men is in charge of the regency.

The desire to occupy an administrative position is an issue that bears no relationship to the position of the regent. If, to entice young men to join the native administration one could tell him that he will certainly become regent, there would be a flood of applicants. The problem is that in the upper levels of indigenous society there is an effort to acquire as much higher education as possible. One attends the *AMS* and *HBS* and continues through college, not with the purpose to practice a trade or profession, but with the aim to gain knowledge, knowledge that conforms to one's talents. There is, at present, little interest in the *hoofdenscholen*. Many persons now become engineers, lawyers, or doctors without considering whether there is a need for such positions. However, the number of candidates for the *hoofdscholen* will increase when the sons of regents receive a university training, provided they are assured of an adequate livelihood.

. . . I meant, with my expression that the *controleur* followed the regent like a shadow, only that the former was inseparable from the latter. This applied only to administrative and economic matters. This was demonstrated by the custom of addressing letters jointly to the regent and *controleur,* who jointly replied to them. This was because of the low educational level of the regents in former days. I recall that, in an old archive, I found documents that spanned a period of several decades, where the advice of the regent to the *controleur* invariably was: "Whatever you say, friend." At the time the regents themselves felt that they had not yet mastered the new conditions and might explain their attempts to provide better training for their sons. Even now the regents consider their education insufficient. They regard higher education as a necessity.

The *controleur* can assume much of the spadework of the regent. Later much of his work was transferred to the district heads. . . . In the transition period of emancipation it was the custom to place, depending on the subject, either the regent's or the *controleur* 's name first on the joint address.

One of the reasons for the decreased contact of the regent with the population is that the educational level of native officials is different from that of the population. Their whole life has changed. I recall a colleague's speech in the People's Council about the days of the present regents' grandfathers. Although they went on tour only twice a year, there was more of a bond with the people, and they were better informed. Now one makes visits once a week and is not well-informed. In the olden days, life was so very different. The regent had relatives throughout the regency, and he amused himself with the population, hunted, and fished, and on such occasions he heard of everything that had taken place. One cannot expect the present regent to return to the former way of life; but contact must be stimulated in a more erudite fashion.

Some time ago I pleaded for including anthropology and sociology courses in the training of native officials, but the former director of *BB* would not hear of this. Yet it is necessary to cultivate, in the officials, a scholarly interest in the population.

. . . a different division of provinces will . . . bring little change in the regents' position. However, one should guard against joining regencies. The communist-instigated revolts, in late 1926,[9] in Banten, were clearly raging most fiercely in the part of the regency Pandeglang that was formerly the separate regency Tjaringin; quite understandably, for there the old regent of Pandeglang had the least personal connections. Joining may be economically advantageous, but otherwise disadvantageous.

As far as the supervision by the European administration is concerned, by the establishment of the regency councils the European officials asked: How will we be informed in the future, if we are losing leadership? But what does one want? Autonomy? Or keeping leadership forever? If one wants to give the regents freedom, one should be able to accept the consequences. There are other forms of supervision. When a decision violative of the general interest or existing regulations has been made, what objection could be raised to having the resident alert the regent, who will be the person who will listen.

Control over the *desa* has nothing to do with the regency council. The assembly of delegates only accepts or rejects the *desa* budget, and the *desa* may appeal to the council of deputies in the province. But why cannot the *controleur* work for the regent and study the *desa*? I do not know why this could not be possible, because the *desa* is a training school. . . . If the assistant resident (new style) is assigned to the regent, he could visit the *desa* everyday. . . .

I did not mean that a *controleur* would only perform office work for the regent, also he should cooperate on the total job. This could lead to a very pleasant relationship, and the regent thus would acquire an indispensable assistant. Local control over the regency council is desirable. Who but the regent is better informed of the local situation? In contrast to the European official he is there all his life. . . .

I readily admit that in the field police we have a modern, well-equipped force. I did not want to make the field police completely subservient to the regent. I have objected to the fact that the regent, although responsible, lacks the power to maintain safety. Incidentally the field police is not totally centrally organized but is placed under local department heads, namely, the residents. I acknowledge wholeheartedly that they function splendidly.

NOTES

1. From: *Handelingen van het Indisch Genootschap,* pp. 83–104. Dutch title: "De positie van de Regenten op Java en Madoera in het huidige bestuurstelsel". Djajadiningrat delivered this lecture at a meeting of the Indisch Genootschap on November 15, 1929.
2. B. J. O. Schrieke in his *Indonesian Sociological Studies, I* (The Hague: W. van Hoeve, 1956), pp. 187–221, analyzes the role of the regents.
3. C. Snouck Hurgronje in his *Verspreide Geschriften, IV, 2.* (Leipzig: Schroeder, 1924), pp. 149–168, recommended emancipating the regents.
4. An umbrella was a status symbol (a relic of the days of the Hindu empires); its use was carefully regulated. In the early twentieth century the colonial government abolished its use as a symbol of rank and class.
5. J. C. Baud, colonial minister and governor-general in the 1840s.
6. *Hoofdenscholen,* schools for chiefs, were established in 1878 for the training of native officials, but attendance was not mandatory.
7. The mayor in the Netherlands is appointed by the government and is not elected by the people in his municipality.
8. This part of the article deals with answers to questions posed after Djajadiningrat delivered his lecture.
9. Referring to the communist instigated revolts in Banten in late 1926.

PART II
THE REFORMERS

W. K. Tehupeiory:
Ambonese Spokesman for the New Elite
(1883-1946)

Although W. K. Tehupeiory was not the first Indonesian to speak out against the treatment of the *doktor djawa* and the conditions under which they worked, as a Christian Ambonese he was more likely than previous advocates to encounter a receptive audience among the Netherlanders.

The population of Ambon had for centuries been under western influence and rule; by the end of the nineteenth century the majority was Christianized, and through the efforts of the missionaries the literacy rate on the island was high. The Ambonese were proud people who considered themselves brown Dutchmen, but they expected to be rewarded for their loyalty to the colonial ruler.

W. K. Tehupeiory was born and grew up in Ambon, where he attended a public school. In 1896 with his older brother he left for Batavia to study at the school for *doktor djawa.* Training was free, but admission requirements were very strict and selective. Tehupeiory was graduated in 1902. After completing several years of service for the colonial government in Java and Sumatra, he went to the Netherlands to secure his Dutch medical certificate.

The opportunity for native physicians to continue their education in the Netherlands was new. The efforts of a *doctor djawa,* Abdul Rivai, who had sought admission to Dutch universities in vain, finally resulted in the regulation that native physicians, after a year and a half of successful study, could obtain a Dutch medical certificate.

Tehupeiory was a reformer who had no desire to change society by force. Until his death he remained loyal to the colonial cause. But he had an acute sense of social justice and the plight and poverty of the common people greatly concerned him. His interest in education and better educational facilities prompted him to establish in 1908 a study fund for needy Ambonese.[1] The colonial government valued his comments and requested his advice on higher education in the Indies. Tehupeiory submitted a proposal in which he elaborated on the need for more and better medical training.

As so many of the intellectual elite of his day he tried his hand at politics. In 1929 with his old friend Dr. Apituley, a member of the People's Council, he formed the Moluccas Political Alliance to offset the influence of the Sarekat Ambon which had openly advocated Indonesian independence. The aims of the alliance were to promote the emancipation of the Moluccas and to secure their autonomy without severing ties with the Netherlands; to support other ethnic groups in the archipelago in their attempts to obtain autonomy; and to establish a federation with other parties in the archipelago.[2] It was a program that attracted few members, and the alliance suffered a languid existence. As a politician Tehupeiory was not a great success.

But he served the people in other ways. Until his death in 1946 he practiced medicine in Djakarta. His patients included rich Chinese living in splendor in their teak-furnished houses behind high walls and well-to-do and less well-to-do Dutch burghers. But his chauffeured Citroen also took him to the *kampongs*, to the Glodok Chinese and to the homes of the poor *Indos*, all of whom were treated free of charge.[3]

Tehupeiory cannot be called a nationalist or a paladin of the nationalist cause. But he was an effective spokesman for the newly emerging elite and an able advocate for better education. Now he is forgotten. But in the hearts of all whose lives he touched, he left an indelible mark.

NOTES

1. "Reorganizatie van het onderwijs aan de school voor opleiding van Inlandsche Artsen te Weltevreden," *Indische Gids* 1909, II, pp. 922–929.
2. J. T. P. Blumberger, *De Nationalistische Beweging in Nederlandsch Indie* (Haarlem: Tjeenk Willink, 1931), pp. 303–304.
3. Dr. Tehupeiory was a long-time friend of my father's and our family doctor in Batavia.

Editor's Introduction:
In Defense of the School for Indonesian Physicians

W. K. Tehupeiory delivered this lecture on January 28, 1908, at the Indies Society (Indisch Genootschap) in The Hague. The impetus was provided by two previous lectures given at the society, one on February 12, 1907 by Dr. J. H. F. Kohlbrugge who spoke on the medical help available to the native population; the other on March 26, 1907 by Mr. Scherp, who lectured on the training of native doctors and, in particular, on the formation of their moral values. The Scherp lecture conveyed a highly pejorative impression not only of the school for *doktor djawa* but of the moral concepts of the students as well. Although Mr. J. H. Abendanon, a former director of the Department of Education in the Indies, sent a letter to the society to try to dispel some of the adverse comments made, Tehupeiory, who read excerpts of the lecture while still in the Indies, felt called upon to outline the conditions at the school. He also took the opportunity to suggest ways for the improvement of the training and the position of the native physician.

The Native Physicians[1]

It is my intention to convey as accurately as possible the conditions under which the native physician works. I also shall provide a description of the peculiar relationship existing between the native doctor and European society, so that a better opinion may be formed about our group than could be obtained from the lectures [that criticized the *doktors djawa*]. Subsequently I shall try to sketch the problems which confront the native doctor in his practice, and I shall speak about the psychological consequences of the struggle for existence. Finally I shall indicate ways in which, according to my colleagues and me, improvements in the existing conditions can be effected.

However, I would like to start by describing school life, whereby it will become evident that the division of the institution into a medical and a preparatory part will not attain the goal . . . envisioned.[2]

Let us consider the newly arrived boys. Mr. Scherp says of them:

> Upon their arrival at the school most of the native youngsters are agreeable, nice boys. Every class gives the impression of a pleasant group. The newcomers are regarded with approval by the new teachers for they are polite in their manners and unassuming in their behavior. Yet the teacher wonders what will become of many of the pupils; how many will be lost to the school—or worse—because of the unfavorable environment in which they are brought.

Indeed, boys between twelve and fourteen are often engaging; they are still nice children, innocent and naive. The school admits students between the ages of twelve and seventeen. During class hours these boys share classrooms, they sleep together in one dormitory and, during the first few months, have little contact with the pupils of the higher grades, with the exception of those who have relatives or friends among the older students . . . .

Because leisure time is generally spent in the dormitories . . . there is little contact between the students of the higher and lower grades; whereas in the recreation room they have to be fully dressed, in the dormitories they can be in their nightclothes. It is a fact that the older students only in exceptional cases will visit the younger ones.

It is . . . my intention to clarify the conditions of life in the *doktor djawa* school for young men from ages twelve to twenty-five. Conditions are not such that they exert a destructive influence on the newly admitted students.

According to me the greatest danger does not come from the students of the higher grades, but from the newcomers who are fifteen and sixteen or reach this age within the year. The majority of the pupils have not yet gone through puberty, however, in the tropics the fifteen- and sixteen-year olds are physically already men. Because they are all classmates, it is the older freshmen who often exert a destructive influence on the younger students. For they live with and among the younger students and by sheer physical force alone may exercise power over the twelve- and thirteen-year olds. Consider, moreover, that no law forces natives to register births; therefore, it will be that often boys obviously seventeen or eighteen are admitted whose reported ages are much lower. Thus, in my first year, I was in the same class with boys who later appeared to have been older than eighteen.

For this reason I do not see any advantage in . . . the separation of the preparatory division and the medical school. . . . For the contact between the young men of twelve and those fifteen and older will continue. . . . The argument that the boys quit school because they remain too long in the same institution seems to me too farfetched. . . .

Let us now examine the influence that the *kampong* has had on the students. Because meals are not provided in the school, the students must eat outside. A minority of them have relatives in Batavia who take care of them, but the majority eat at the home of strangers, often former (expelled) students who have found a position in Batavia and have married *kampong* women.

Shortly after one o'clock the students leave for the *kampong* to have their lunch; afterward the majority return to school, but a few, those who have known their host for some time, relax for a short nap rather than make the return trip in the burning sun. They wait until the greatest heat has subsided and then they return. They have brought their books to their host's home, but they will rarely touch them. All afternoon they are pleasantly entertained by their host and his family. I need not emphasize that the conversation will be in Javanese or Malay. Some of the students remain in the *kampong* until just before their evening assignments. On Sundays these same students remain at their host's all day long and return only just before the evening roll call.

Why do some of the students still like to stay in the *kampong* when the school is so well equipped and offers so many opportunities for relaxation? Earlier I made some passing remarks that the heat makes the students shrink back from returning to school so soon after their meal. Another reason is music. For those familiar with the *pantuns* and *stambul* songs and who have heard them interpreted on the guitar, who know the stirring character of these songs, especially when played in the moonlight which in the Indies is delightful, should not be surprised that a susceptible newcomer will be profoundly moved and will require great willpower to return to school where only prosaic lessons await him.

Add to this the little usually uplifting scenes often enacted in the *kampong* and you will understand why this life has a destructive influence on the students. . . . The student who has no relatives in Batavia is entirely on his own; however, I should emphasize that the older students unconsciously exercise a great positive influence and many, realizing the threatening danger for the younger ones, often sound warnings.

While the students lived at home there was always a higher authority—the parents'—no matter how lightly enforced. At school, after the lessons, he is free. Because of the great freedom he has suddenly acquired, he kicks over the traces; in the beginning he is still subdued and shy toward the older students, later he becomes bolder for there is no one who will scold him for his behavior. The important question here is, was the upbringing at home such that it conveyed the realization that freedom must be enjoyed in a restrained manner?

The majority of the native children are indeed very spoiled, especially in the higher social classes where they are surrounded by a retinue of servants, who attend the child at his beck and call and condone everything. From childhood on they always want their way, and parental indulgence hardens them in their inclinations . . . the student usually does not improve after one year in school. The daily supervision by the two caretakers is purely regulatory and does not provide the students with better ideas and concepts. Often such boys will go astray, but others do not because their ambition is stimulated by the progress of their fellow students. The root of evil generally lies at home . . . attempts to bring about changes will produce results only after decades. At present all that can be done is to prevent students from visiting the *kampong*.

We have seen that the young men are forced to go to the *kampong* because the school does not provide meals. If we could serve meals at the school, the necessity for visiting the *kampong* will be eliminated. Only those who have friends and acquaintances will occasionally go to the *kampong*, but even this will occur less often.

How is it possible that we still find many native physicians who perform their duty, in fact, more than their duty, despite these less favorable conditions prevailing before and during the school years? that among the graduates we find people who according to the testimony of many doctors have great compassion for the deprived?

So many virtues are taught in medical education; in every case of illness there is a search for the truth. Here kudos to the teachers—army physicians—are in order, for, by their good example, they exhort the students to perform good deeds and without fanfare inculcate social graces.

For the efficient operation of the school, permanent teachers are imperative . . . in my second year of study I had four physiology teachers in one year. Nearly every year many teachers are transferred which invariably means a disruption of education.

At present teaching is a part-time job for the army physician; only during class hours does he see the institution. . . . More interest in the school and in the students will be required of the teachers, when meals provided in the institution will obviate the trip to the *kampong*. Then the boys need to be kept busy during the afternoon, and the teacher could perform a very useful function by participating in games. . . .

Through this informal contact with their educators, the boys could learn a great deal; unobtrusively they will be taught good manners; their ideas and opinions will be changed for the better.

It is regrettable that presently only two permanent teachers are connected with the school. The appointment of permanent teachers is imperative for the sake of the school. . . .

Under the present circumstances, for the native medical school, I consider the appointment of a resident nurse sufficient rather than a resident physician, as had been suggested. She could teach nursing and devote her spare time to tending to the boys. And the sick will receive better care than a teacher's wife can give.

It appears to me . . . that the teachers, even though not in residence, can contribute a great deal to the character formation of the students. Although according to the regulations only the director and the two supervisors are in charge of the young men after school hours, in my opinion, this should not prevent the teacher from doing what he considers necessary for the moral education of the boys. Even though in most schools it is certainly the task of the teachers to keep the parents abreast of the progress of the children, this is not possible at the native medical school. The students are recruited from all parts of the archipelago; a correspondence of dubious value would have to be carried out. Instead is it such a sacrifice to show interest in the student associations a few times a week or to invite the students to one's home and amuse them with games and the like? How easy then it would be for the best students to become acquainted with boys from influential families.

Previously I mentioned *kampong* life as the principal cause of the failure of many often-bright students. However, there are other reasons which take away the desire to study . . . , and one can . . . understand why so many native medical doctors leave government service. To give an example: of the nine graduates in 1906, three have already submitted their resignation.

Until 1898 the salary of *doktor djawa* was fifty guilders a month. Native physicians are entitled to travel second class on *KPM* ships and third class by train. [In these rights] They are on an equal level with the *mantri;* for day trips they receive one guilder and reimbursement for travel expenses when traveling more than six *palen* [over eleven kilometers] from their residence.

The *doktor djawa* acquires all these rights after completing grade school, as one of the top students, and seven, long years of difficult study. Is it surprising that the Ambonese student, after a few years in school and enlarging his knowledge of Dutch, with the prospect of such a salary seeks another position, primarily that of clerk, for which he (with his Dutch and his intellect) will receive thirty guilders and which opens the possibility of becoming a customs—and thus a European—official.

Especially annoying was the thought that a *doktor djawa* was always treated and considered as an ordinary native, while as the lowest clerk he was considered a European if legally accepted as equal.[3] This situation still prevails, although to a lesser extent; the European condescends less often to the educated native and similarly, we the students of the *doktor djawa* school no longer feel ashamed to be natives. I do not think that there is one clerk now who deems himself above the *doktor djawa*, solely because he belongs to the ruling race, even though his skin color would not indicate this.[4] I shall cite an example which shows that well-to-do *Indo* families even now regard the native, no matter how well trained or brought up, as an inferior creature. A native doctor who had a flourishing practice among European officials, delighted in the confidence that he enjoyed among these families (nearly all Eurasians). He was invited to parties, participated in all events, and was completely regarded as a housefriend. At one time he suggested starting a tennis club, a plan acclaimed by all those present. Guess what happened then? The tennis club was started without him, in fact, he was even excluded. The reason was obviously this: one could not be expected to play on a tennis court with a native. It stands to reason that, if a European official feels ashamed to show himself publicly in the company of the native doctor, a constructive relationship is not possible.

Is the influence of the low remuneration, already evident during the school years, indicated by the high dropout rate? This becomes even more apparent when the *doktor djawa*, armed with his diploma, enters the world. Here he is able to compare himself with other officials, European as well as native, and inevitably other positions appear more enticing. It is true that in 1898 the salary was raised from fifty to seventy guilders, and the maximum pay from ninety to one hundred fifty guilders, but this by a long shot is not sufficient for the *doktor djawa*.[5]

Let us first examine what the *doktor djawa* has to perform for the stated salary and rights. Because I am naturally most familiar with the work that I did when I was a native physician, I shall take the liberty to use this as an example.

I was in charge of public health care in the subdistrict of Medan [East Coast of Sumatra] . . . . treating the ill in the men's hospital, with an average of seventy patients, in the women's and leper hospitals . . . each averaging twenty; in addition every morning during weekdays, there was outpatient care in the men's hospital and that averaged about twenty people daily. I also had to go to the jails for sick calls, on an average of ten cases a day.

I was also in charge of the medical examination of prostitutes: about forty Japanese and Klingalese came on Tuesdays and Saturdays and about a hundred Chinese came on Thursdays.

In addition I was the legal coroner, [a position] which often involved considerable work for I had to assist the magistrate with written advice and information . . . three times a week and that took much of my time. Once a week I had to go to the village of Sunggal—a distance of more than three and a half *palen* [over six kilometers] for medical care of the population.

I was also entrusted with the care of sixty Chinese in the Chinese-supported hospital; for this I received an additional fifty guilders.

This was my work under normal circumstances. During epidemics (*in casu* cholera) I was expected to disinfect contaminated houses and public buildings, such as jails and schools; then I often had to go to the various Batak villages which were sometimes separated by twenty *palen* [thirty-seven kilometers] . . . .

Such a heavy schedule is by no means an exception. In several places of Java, *doktors djawa* are entrusted with outpatient care and the supervision of prostitutes in distant villages within their jurisdiction. Besides, after sundown the work is not ended for one is often awakened by emergencies: judicial and insanity cases.

Most regulations concerning *doktors djawa* in the Indies apply to the entire archipelago, only rarely will they be modified to meet local needs. That would entail too much trouble. And, if eventually a change is effected, an incomplete job is done and many categories of officials are forgotten. Thus when travel regulations were changed European officials with a salary of three hundred guilders or more could travel first class free, while lower-ranking officials, clerks, and enlisted men were entitled to free second-class travel. The *mantri* police, yes, even the auctioneer could travel second class, but the *doktor djawa* has only free third-class travel.

To understand the situation, one must realize that the *mantri* police are recruited from among the best native writers or wardens. They are charged with the preliminary investigation in district court cases. The auctioneers are native scribes who lead the bidding at auctions. Neither they nor the *mantri* police know Dutch, and their education consists of the completion of a native grade school.

I am sure you will agree that we owe it to our position to travel at least second class (for only coolies and prisoners travel third class) but under the present regulations, we had to pay the additional expense from our own minimal remuneration. The daily reimbursement for expenses one receives in addition to the transportation costs amounts to one guilder; but usually we receive only half a guilder, for we try to return to our post the same day, especially if we want to work in the hospital the next day. As you may know only half of the daily expenses allowed is refunded when we do not spend the night in another city. This amount is naturally not enough to defray additional travel costs, not to mention the transportation costs for a carriage from the station to the hospital. At my repeated insistence and after a formal request to the resident, the travel regulations for native doctors in Deli [East Sumatra] were finally changed.[6]

In 1904 the government addressed a notice to the head of the regional administration to see to it that the native medical doctors were properly rewarded for special services and to secure their cooperation to combat abuses, if this was necessary. Nonetheless it indeed occurred that a secretary [of a regional administrator] requested a *doktor djawa* to appear officially in his office to reproach the *doktor djawa* for sending a bill to a European who was not entitled to free medical treatment. Only after the *doktor djawa*, in a written reply, alerted the secretary to the regulation and had thus shown his action was proper, was the bill paid.

Previously I mentioned that in 1898 the starting salary was raised to seventy guilders and the maximum salary, after twelve years of service, to one hundred fifty guilders. Free housing is provided in only two or three cases. In Batavia an insufficient indemnity for rent is given, so one can afford only a house deep in the *kampong*. Because of his position the native physician cannot live in a boarding house like other unmarried young officials. While on house calls to the native population, clothes get dirty quickly, for, besides dressing wounds he often has to sit on dirty benches or mats. The native physician has to spend much more than the ordinary official for clothes and laundry, because by practicing the greatest possible hygiene he will be an example to the natives, with whom he is in daily contact.

In Java for decent meals, he will easily have to pay forty guilders a month, in the outer provinces [outside Java] this is considerably higher. Little is left of his salary, for his rent amounts to twenty guilders, one servant costs six, then only four guilders remain: just enough to pay the laundry.

Then he still has to furnish his home comfortably, and last but not least pay for newspapers, journals, and books. These are the expenses for the bachelor, but what problems the married native physician faces, one can figure out by simple calculation.

... It is easy to accuse the *doktor djawa* that he has no compassion for his fellowmen, but I would like to invite everyone to examine how a *doktor djawa* lives with his family, to consider how he has to slave, after enervating work for the government, to cover his deficit with additional income from his private practice.[7]

Would he, who exerts himself for a sick Chinese, not hasten to treat his compatriot if the *doktor djawa* could enjoy an adequate salary and be free from financial worries? It is no feat, when one earns more than enough, to treat several thousand natives free of charge, that is simply all in a day's work. But it is laudable when, in straitened circumstances, one readily helps the poor.

Do not think the native physician can completely live as any other native official. After a nine-year stay at the school he has become accustomed to European surroundings, and it is with this model in mind that he will later furnish his home. He has, just as a European official, a need for books and music, and he wants his children to attend a good European school. All this he must try to pay for from his minimal salary.

If he should fall ill he will receive only one month's full salary; after that he will be put on half pay or be dismissed. Like all other native officials a *doktor djawa* will receive a pension after thirty years of uninterrupted service. After his death, his wife and offspring cannot expect anything. What European official would, under such circumstances, continue his devotion to the service? What group would so long have accepted these conditions?

Add to all this the fact that the *doktor djawa* may be transferred to the most distant areas . . . , whereby he invariably takes a loss in the sale of his furniture and household goods. I have now mentioned all the circumstances in pleading for an increment in salary.

Not in the training nor in the peculiar eastern ideas should one search for the cause of his [the Native physician] small concern for his fellow countryman, but in the fact that the native physician is paid too little and is often treated unfairly. Is it surprising that he becomes more and more indifferent in the fulfillment of his duties . . . but some of the blame should be attributed to the insufficient supervision of the superiors, the administrative officials, and the civil physician.

These men should exercise influence on the further development of the *doktor djawa*. . . . They are given a very difficult task for knowing the personality and character of their subordinate is a prerequisite for their [the *doktors djawa*'s] future success.

The European physician, in particular, should regard him [the *doktor djawa*] more as a colleague. We have too much respect for the greater knowledge of the European physician that this friendship could harm the latter's status. . . . In conversations the European physician can impart much of his ideas on duty, philanthropy, determination, and so on. Mr. Kohlbrugge asserts that it is impossible to imbue a man of the tropics with these concepts. I cannot believe this.

May I point to the flourishing associations, both in Ambon and in Batavia, to support widows and orphans and to assist compatriots? May I point out the energy and the sense of duty of the military police? This force, the pick of the native and Ambonese soldiers, performs tasks highly enervating to Europeans in the long run, and therefore is performed with lesser results than when done by a native soldier who is equipped with a considerable sense of detective instinct and other characteristics.

As a military policeman he considers himself higher than an ordinary soldier, whether European or native. He is not only in name but in fact valued more, as evidenced by his higher pay. He is ready, at any moment to show that he merits the distinction; he does his utmost and often demonstrates leadership which, previously, no one expected of him.

The native wants recognition for his good characteristics, if this is not forthcoming he will become resigned and indifferent. On the other hand, one should guard against excessive praise which may easily make him reckless and cause him to lose respect for officials. Thus serious shortcomings among the native doctors should be instantly and severely punished. . . . Effective punishment has great educational value also for the native doctor.

. . . the newly graduated native physician should have supervision, but this should be carried out with great tact. . . . No trace of suspicion should be present in the words of the superior; on the contrary everything should exude trust. Indeed a very difficult task, but only thus can one produce a group of people who can later serve in positions of leadership.

And according to me, this is the goal we should attain. In summary, I consider it indispensable for the school and the profession to:

1) Provide meals at the school
2) Hire a sick nurse
3) Hire permanent teachers
4) Improve treatment of the native medical doctors by European officials
5) Provide better and adequate remuneration for native physicians

. . . a sufficient salary will enable them to gain access to higher social circles, and they can thus cultivate what they have learned, shielding them from less courteous treatment by Europeans. . . .

The position of the native physicians is indeed unique. Upon assignment they are in charge of treating those Europeans who earn less than one hundred and fifty guilders. Because of their work they come into more contact with Europeans than with any other group of native officials, even though some may have studied Dutch and received a European education. Moreover, the native physician is under the supervision of the local European administratior, so that he has less contact with native chiefs than any of the other native officials. He is not pressured as much to observe the *adat*, is freer and can behave more like an European official.[8] For that reason he is more likely to associate with the European official. . . .

. . . we must seek out the friends of the *doktor djawa* in better circles, and these are among the postal employees, supervisors, and teachers. But here we encounter a stumbling block. The way of life of these European officials and that of the native physician differ too much; only if the native doctors earn a higher salary could there be more social contact with the European officials.

If the native doctor is to participate in the spiritual life of the educated families, then in my opinion it is important that he keeps abreast of current events by reading his [medical] journals and thus practice his Dutch constantly. . . .

The fear that, when he receives a higher salary, he will become alienated from the group of which he is a part is groundless; when he is in a financially independent position he will find more time for the dedicated treatment of the natives. Now he often has to set aside time for private patients for they provide him with the money he needs for a living. . . . Especially now that the native doctors are admitted to the theoretical examinations at the university, an indication that they are more accurately evaluated, a salary discrepancy is no longer justified.[9]

That a future salary revision favors the native physician over the *doktor djawa* is not only desirable but an incentive for further study by the latter. Not only is this fair, but it will also provide the *doktor djawa* with a stimulus to study obstetrics.[10] For what is now the situation? The *doktor djawa* sees no financial advantage in studying obstetrics because as a native physician he will receive the same salary. As *doktor djawa*, he can assist parturient women if he is the only doctor stationed in a post.

Our beginning salary is certainly too low. . . . After nine years of study, a starting salary of one hundred fifty guilders is certainly not too much, considering that out of this the rent for a good house needs to be paid. The maximum salary should be fixed at three hundred guilders after reaching twelve years of service. The *doktor djawa* who received the old education should receive a maximum of two hundred guilders.

For the daily expense and the transportation costs by land and sea rules similar to those of European officials should apply . . . . Of the utmost importance are regulations for payment in case of illness and pensions for widows and orphans so that the present uncertain situation is terminated.

With this lecture I wanted to provide you with a glimpse of the life of the *doctor djawa*, especially his position in the European community and to inform you about his work and his status.

Thus far Europeans have been our spokesmen and the salary increase . . . was almost entirely accomplished by our director alone. I felt, therefore, that the opinion of one who had worked as a native physician could be of use.

I would feel adequately rewarded, if, by this lecture, I had elicited an interest in the group of which I once was a part, an interest that I hope will bring about improvement in the position of the native physician.

NOTES

1. This translation is made from the article "Iets over de Inlandsche Geneeskundigen," *Handelingen van het Indisch Genootschap* (1908): 101-121. This version is abbreviated.

2. The school for *doktor djawa* was founded in 1851 and offered in the beginning a two-year training program for vaccinators who, during epidemics, could assist in the immunization of the population. The study program was steadily expanded; by 1875 the school was divided into a two-year preparatory division and a five-year medical program. In 1902 the school was reorganized and the complete program encompassed nine years of training. The old *doktor djawa* school then became the School for Training of Native Physicians (STOVIA). *Ontwikkeling van het Geneeskundig Onderwijs in Weltevreden* (Weltevreden:Kolff, 1926), pp. 1-30.
3. The law made a distinction between Dutch citizens and Dutch subjects (the latter included most of the native Indonesian population). Christian Indonesians and most educated Indonesians were so-called equalized (in Dutch *gelijkgesteld*). This way they acquired some of the rights and duties of Europeans and were tried in a European rather than a native court.
4. Tehupeiory here refers to Eurasians (called *Indos*) who, although many were indistinguishable from the Indonesians in the color of their skin, were considered Europeans under the law.
5. On the recommendation of Christiaan Snouck Hurgronje the salary of the *doktor djawa* was increased and some of the work conditions improved. E. Gobée and C. Adriaanse, eds., *Ambtelijke Adviezen van C. Snouck Hurgronje* (The Hague: Nijhoff, 1956), Part II, pp. 1040-1046.
6. Dutch administrative official who was head of a residency, in rank below governor.
7. *Doktors djawa* were permitted to treat private patients. The majority of their patients were Chinese, and in posts where no European physician was stationed, Europeans and Eurasians.
8. The constant flouting of *adat* by the Indonesian physicians and their habit of wearing European clothing aroused the ire of many Indonesian officials, in particular on Java. C. Snouck Hurgronje, *Verspreide Geschriften* (Leipzig: Schroeder, 1924), 4, no. 2, pp. 35-43.
9. In 1904 the graduates of the School for Training of Native Physicians were admitted to the theoretical examination of the medical faculties in the Netherlands and, after a year and a half of study, could receive their Dutch medical degree. Robert van Niel, *The Emergence of the Modern Indonesian Elite* (The Hague: Nijhoff, 1960), p. 52.
10. With the establishment of the STOVIA, courses in obstetrics became mandatory.

Hadji Agus Salim

Hadji Agus Salim: Modern Moslem
(1884-1954)

The wispy old man with a white goatee, dubbed the "Grand Old Man" of the Indonesian nationalist movement, hailed from the Minangkabau area in Sumatra.[1] Salim, born on October 8, 1884, was the son of a *hoofddjaksa*. He attended a Dutch grade school in Sumatra and then departed for Batavia enrolling in the King William III high school, where he graduated third in a class of thirty-five.

At the recommendation of C. Snouck Hurgronje, Advisor of Native Affairs who for years had advocated sending an Indonesian to Jidda to work at the Dutch Consulate, Salim was appointed to the position. Snouck's evaluation of Salim has remained for posterity: a very perspicacious young man with a good intellect and a boldness remarkable even for a Malay.[2]

Salim worked for five years in Jidda, learned Arabic and became acquainted with the Islamic modernist movement. After returning to Indonesia he served in various positions: he directed a school, worked as a translator, was editor for a newspaper, and joined the Sarekat Islam. Calling himself a socialist Moslem and asserting that the Koran already advocated socialist principles, he clashed with the communists who had infiltrated the party. Salim succeeded in having party discipline adopted, leading to the purge of Marxist elements. But it also heralded the decline of the party. In 1923, the Sarekat Islam was renamed; its religious foundations reemphasized; and its adherence to Islamic unity stressed.

Salim remained a member of this group until 1936, when his decision to abandon noncooperation with the government led to his expulsion. He then became active in the committee seeking support for the Sutarjo Petition among the Indonesian people. But he declined to support GAPI, the federation of Indonesian political organizations, and also opposed the movement for an Indonesian parliament in 1940.[3]

Salim, who had formed his own party (Pergerakan Penjadar), believed that grassroots democracy should precede a political movement on a national scale. In education, religion, and politics, he sought to cultivate a community spirit by arousing popular awareness of pressing problems at the *kampong* and *desa* levels.[4]

Salim served the colonial government in a number of functions. He was a member of the Revision Commission on the Constitutional Status of the Indies in 1920 and filed a minority report expressing the view that the Indies should have more autonomy and should not be ruled by a country thousands of miles away. From 1921 to 1924 he was a member of the People's Council, where he tried to make his fellow members aware of the social problems confronting Indonesia. He also served as representative with the Dutch delegation at the International Labor Conference in Geneva in 1930.

During the Japanese occupation he worked briefly in the Putera movement, and when Indonesia declared its independence in 1945 he served in a number of cabinet positions. His command of languages (he spoke seven fluently) made him the spokesman par excellence for the country, and he was sent, during the height of the conflict with the Dutch, to India, the Middle East, and New York to plead Indonesia's cause, which he accomplished with great success.

In 1953 he taught a seminar on Islam at Cornell University, and among his graduate students was Harry Benda, who kept fond memories of this remarkable, versatile, and compassionate man.

On the occasion of his seventieth birthday, Salim's friends presented him with a collection of his writings *Djedjak Langkah Hadji Agus Salim*. He died a month later; at his funeral the Indonesian people paid him a moving tribute.

Hadji Agus Salim was a genuine nationalist who wanted to see Indonesia independent. Yet he adhered to his principles, regardless of their popularity and cared little for power per se. As a politician he was simply not pragmatic or unscrupulous enough to be successful. His ideas on Islam were, in some respects, modern yet on such a basic issue as polygamy, he adamantly maintained that it should be preserved because the Koran allowed it. Hadji Agus Salim was a Moslem with socialist sympathies, a man of high principles, who was not willing to forsake his beliefs for the sake of expediency.

NOTES

1. This biographical sketch is based on information from the following publications: D. M. C. Koch, *Batig Slot. Figuren uit het oude Indie* (Amsterdam: De Brug/Djambatan, 1960), pp. 130-138; St. Rais Alamsjah, *10 Orang Indonesia Terbesar Sekarang* (Djakarta: Mutiara, 1952), pp. 119-137; Solinchin Salam, *Hadji Agus Salim* (Djakarta: Djajamurni, 1955).
2. *Ambtelijke Adviezen van Christiaan Snouck Hurgronje* 2, E. Gobée and C. Adriaanse eds., ('S Gravenhage: Nijhoff, 1959), pp. 1949-1950.
3. S. L. van de Wal, *De Volksraad en de Staatkundige Ontwikkeling van Nederlands-Indie* 2, (Groningen: Wolters, 1965), p. 416. Salim was against the GAPI because he feared that the sovereignty of the respective parties would be curtailed. He was for convening a national conference of parties, leaving them free to act as they pleased.
4. Ibid., p. 510.

Editor's Introduction:
The League of Young Moslems

This article was based on a lecture that Hadji Agus Salim delivered at the second convention of the League of Young Moslems held in Solo in December, 1926.

The League of Young Moslems was established in 1925. Among its aims were the promotion of Islam and of Islamic unity. It also favored the development of a viable form of Indonesian nationalism.[1]

The Veiling and Isolation of Women

The "harem" and everything related to it invariably has been, for European readers, a subject, if not of interest at least of curiosity.[2] The depictions of Moslem married life that nearly every cultured European reading popular, travel accounts conjures up are generally wrong. The results of studies by orientalists are falsified because these legends are so widespread; scholars of repute who, having retained these fallacious ideas acquired in their schooldays, are at times led astray even in translating and explaining passages in the Koran, when discussing the influence of Islam on society and family.

Professor Snouck Hurgronje,[3] the most famous of all European Islamic scholars wrote thus in his essay, "Two Popular Fallacies Corrected," which has been recently reissued in Part I of *Collected Writings,* p. 35.

It is important to our Young Moslems and our Indonesian youth in general to be aware of this attestion from such an unexpected source. In particular because the "most erroneous" depictions of "nearly every cultured European" have found acceptance by our "western" educated youth via European "teachers" or "advisers" and also more directly from "reading popular travel accounts and novels" and other disguised Christian or at any rate anti-Islamic propaganda.

It is therefore understandable that I instantly took the opportunity to speak on the veiling and isolation of women at our latest JIB Congress in Solo.

For the information of the readers who did not witness the rather demonstrative action of their association's adviser Salim, I recapitulate. I have noted on several occasions that in JIB circles there is a tendency to consider Islamic that which is the opposite of what is presently pursued by our intellectuals or regarded by them as acceptable. Which is of course wrong.

One manifestation of this tendency is to separate at meeting women and men in the audience. The ladies are then tucked away behind a screen. The ludicrousness of this imitation of the Arabs is more apparent, because the ladies usually arrive frank and free in open carriages without the prescribed headcovering. . . .

In addition, the isolation of ladies at our meetings is far from favorable for the publicity of our association, as understandably among the female intellectual youth, who are participating in the revival of our national consciousness, an arabization of our customs must be far from agreeable. And again the rigorous separation of women is not an Islamic requirement but an Arabic *adat*.

Dr. Th. W. Juynboll states in his *Handbuch des Islamischen Gesetzes:*

> The veiling of the women was long before the coming of Islam a habit in many eastern countries also among the Christians. But in Mohammad's surroundings this was not the case and nothing justifies the supposition, that the Prophet prescribed Moslem women to wear the veil. . . .

Therefore, I felt that I should not shrink from the demonstrative, yes, even, deliberate way of pulling away the *hidjab* (screen) which concealed the women from the men of the audience and blocked their view of the meeting, in the interest of the *Jong Islamieten Bond* and the publicity for a viable Islam in general, in conformity with His highest law, the Koran, and in the spirit and the example of the founder, our venerated Prophet the Lord Emissary Muhammad, may Allah bestow upon him honor and peace.

Our brother Wiwoho gave me the opportunity to explain my action, which I did in a speech and I hereby render from memory—I did not make any notes, nor could I get these from others.[4] Moreover, in the following rendition citations are more extensively used.

Ladies and gentlemen:

I am honored to respond to an invitation of our chairman to explain my action (the removal of the screen segregating the women in the audience). The goal of the League of Young Moslems is to understand and live according to Islam. It is therefore imperative that the League frees itself of all those rules and habits that are not part of Islam and that do not originate from the original teaching of Islam. Therefore, it is necessary that the members of the League of Moslems realize what Allah ordered and what was prescribed by the prophet or was sanctioned by his example. The segregation and even less the isolation of women were not among the sanctioned. That segregation is an Arabic custom does not make it an Islamic requirement. This rule may be part of the belief of Jews and Christians alike, for in these religions, women have been accorded a dependent and subservient position, but this rule is definitively not in accordance with the teaching and the spirit of Islam, which started the emancipation of women, when the Koran was introduced. The Arabs have taken this custom of segregating and veiling women, not from Islam, but from the Jews and Christians before the coming of Islam. It is not surprising that, outside the Arabic countries, this custom has not at all been universally accepted by Islamized people.

Islam leaves no doubt on what is an Islamic requirement. Allah's own word in his holy Koran formulates rules to which men and women should submit. . . .

In the Koran the prescription is, even in detail, explicit enough. It concerns, quite obviously. . . . the appearance of women in public in the presence of strange men and women, outside of the narrower family circle and. . . . those who form part of the family circle. The very existence of this prescription excludes all thought of the enforced seclusion of women, let alone the confinement of women. And nowhere is mentioned the veiling of face and the covering of other parts of the body, except those which may be labelled sexual and are part of the beauty and assets of women.

In his "Two Popular Fallacies Corrected," Snouck remarks in this connection:

> Strictly speaking the rules order women, as far as clothing is concerned, little more than what is considered decent in European society. Women's clothing bears witness to her modesty and chastity; they should avoid arousing all wrong desire by men who see them, they are extremely cautious in their association with all men except their husband, their male relatives with whom they could never marry, their slaves, their servants.

With the exception of the comparison with "European society," which Snouck apparently cannot but regard as "standard"—considering that he wrote this passage and could not forsee how concepts of decency in European society would develop—no one can in all fairness reach any other conclusion. No one can deny with any justification that the prescription entails something more than is strictly necessary for the elevation of women to a higher human and moral level and to maintain their status. The "European woman" with her high moral Christian values, which accord more place to inner values than outer appearances, is an instructive example in alerting mankind that inhibition is indispensable for inner development. As indispensable as outside order and regularity are for the development of self-containment, so is the covering of the body and limitations in the relationship between the sexes indispensable for the development and preservation of modesty, chastity, and high morality.

Some things may be learned . . . . Namely [that] men are instructed to guard their chastity, while women must guard their own. Men did not receive any orders or authorization to appoint themselves as guardians over women's chastity. Only arrogant appropriation in violation of the spirit of Allah's law can lead to a misconception in this respect. A misconception which does not help the problem, for it shortchanges or exaggerates the limitations set by Allah, and these misconceptions lead to the opposite of the intended goal.

Moreover, it must become evident to everyone that men's guardianship over women's chastity is definitely misplaced, because the women must protect themselves precisely from the men's aggression. To give men power in this cannot but be a debasement of women. The requirement in the Koran and the teachings of the honored Prophet—may God bestow honor and peace upon him—do not support this view. Rather the opposite view applies, namely, mothers of believers are entrusted with teaching men chastity. . . .

That higher demands are set for wives of the Prophet, mothers of the faithful, goes without saying, just as the Prophet is the standard example for believing men. But believing women, because they are the mothers and prospective mothers of the believers, have the duty to follow the given example as closely as possible. Only then will menfolk grow up knowing how to live according to the example of the Prophet.

Ladies and gentlemen, I have hereby given a bird's-eye view of the requirements on the body covering of the women and the restrictions in the relationship between the sexes, and I believe I have pointed out that in these regulations there is no reference whatever to the seclusion or segregation of women.

Again I would like to emphasize that none of the regulations supports a "shepherding" of men over women's chastity. If one can speak of influence at all in this regard, this can but be found in those Koran regulations whereby a woman by her attitude and behavior can exercise an influence on men.

I do not wish to terminate without saying a word on "the great lie of the west," which unfortunately is accepted here increasingly. Namely, the lie that marital happiness would be assured by intimate premarital relations, whereby the parties will get to know each other better. Because of this lie—under the slogan "respect for the institution of marriage"—the door is opened wide for a well-nigh limitless freedom in the relationships between young men and young women. Even in situations where there were previously no thoughts of an honest intention of marriage. Indeed most young men do not at all think of marriage when they surrender to undeniable pleasure, found in flirting and dancing, in games and necking, which are part of the free relationship between the sexes. Obviously a more meaningful relationship and well-considered judgment are impossible in a relationship which arouses the senses and is primarily pleasure-seeking.

Besides, relationships on which a harmonious living together should be based can only be achieved in and through marriage . . . . Every honest married man or woman could only testify that to get to know and appreciate the other party will come later in marriage, and this long after the honeymoon; while harmony in marriage comes only after many years. And the chances for this increase, when expectations in the beginning are not as high, and both parties have less of an idealized image of one another. . . .

Yet Islam does not require that the man and the woman should marry "unseen."

On the contrary! For convenience's sake I shall again refer to Snouck's article:

> The Sjafi'ites not only consider permissible that the husband views his prospective wife but *"sonna"* and desired by God. Even if the woman herself or he, who is her guardian refuses a man this opportunity of "viewing", he, who contemplates asking for a woman's hand in marriage has the right to seize every opportunity presenting itself to see her. "It is sufficient for him to have the permission of the Highest Lawgiver" as the scholars express this, and he can dispense with the rules of men. He can even repeat viewing her as often as he deems necessary to come to a serious decision. Again: such an insistence on personal acquaintance before marriage ill-befits a law which would require all women to move about in society veiled (p. 311).

I would like to finish with a serious word to the Islamic youth in general and the Young Moslems in particular.

Our nation is in a position which is far from honorable. A great deal needs to be improved in our feelings of self-esteem, in our regard for ourselves and for our nation. This improvement is impossible if we do not start putting our girls and mothers—the future and present mothers of our nation—on a pedestal, a place accorded them by God and His Prophet. Therefore, let our young men never approach a woman other than with respect, which she deserves, and if she does not, which she will need to elevate herself. Never consider a girl or woman an object of amusement, not even a comrade with whom you can have fun or go out.

If your nature urges you to take a wife seek then honestly the advice of parents or friends in whom you can trust. When they suggest someone to whom you might be attracted then approach her honorably and openly with the intention of marriage.

If you consider marriage now impossible then, according to the teachings of the Koran, seek recourse in prayer and fasting. Protect yourself from your own nature, by prudence and simplicity of lifestyle, and abstain from seeking satisfaction for your pressing desires by flirting.

It demeans you as well as the girls and women with whom you associate, even though you may pretend, by respectable behavior, to place her on a high pedestal. It impairs your sense of self-esteem and destroys your respect for girls and women in general, which will also become an obstacle for the development of your nationalist conscience toward your own people.

I also have some advice for and request to the ladies and girls of our Young Moslems. No matter how appealing the position of a "modern" woman may appear, your inner nature cannot deceive you on true values, if only you recognize reality . . . . Those who honestly and sincerely seek the truth will undoubtedly find it.

In the preceding article I have referred, more frequently and extensively than in the speech delivered on the subject, to statements by Professor Snouck Hurgronje for valuable testimony from him on Islam are of exceptional value as this is an "Islam expert par excellence" who only rarely passes up an opportunity to belittle Islam and who, in his judgments and conclusions, freely asserts his justly famed acrimony and acuity.

The possibility that he would give a flattering (that is, a pretty) picture is thus absent. I can, therefore, with confidence, offer the preceding statements to the Islamic young people as a reliable compass on which they can easily rely as far as the relationship between the sexes according to Islam is concerned. May they be good and beneficial to many. Amen!

NOTES

1. J. Th. Petrus Blumberger, *De Nationalistische Beweging in Nederlandsch Indie* (Haarlem: Tjeenk Willink, 1931), pp. 402–403.
2. *Djedjak Langkah Hadji A. Salim* (Djakarta: Tintamas, 1954), pp. 167–175. Original Dutch title: "De sluiering en afzondering van de vrouw," published in *Het Light* (1926). Translated with permission of the publisher Tintamas and the heirs of H. A. Salim.
3. C. Snouck Hurgronje was Advisor of Native Affairs from 1889 until 1906. From 1907 until his retirement in 1927, he taught Arabic at the University of Leyden. He was a noted Islamic scholar.
4. Raden Wiwoho Purbohadidjojo was chairman of the League of Young Moslems and later (1931–1942) was a member of the People's Council, where he was allied with the Nationalist Faction.

Editor's Introduction:
Coolie Legislation and the Penal Sanction

The big plantations established at the close of the nineteenth century needed, to insure maximum profitability, a supply of cheap and readily available labor. Sumatra, where the largest plantations existed, was sparsely populated thus it became imperative to recruit workers either from the Straits Settlements (Chinese coolies) or from Java. However, in the colonial era the Javanese was a poor immigrant.

The first coolie legislation dates from the 1890s and was enacted entirely in the interest of the employer.[1] It proscribed the laborer from breaking his contract and provided for legal action by the employer to enforce the employer's rights. It was thus a form of servitude.

In 1923 when changes in the coolie legislation were debated in the People's Council, a group of four members (Salim was one of them) proposed abolition of the hated penal code, which they described as covert slavery. They had very little support. Even a rather enlightened man as Achmad Djajadiningrat considered the penal sanction a necessary evil which had to do until an alternative was found.

The explanation provided by the government for maintaining the penal sanction was that:

1. The prosperity of the Outer Provinces would be dealt a serious blow.

2. Elimination of the penal code would mean a reduction in profit of at least 26 million guilders, considered too high at the existing productivity level.

3. All regional district heads were against abolition.

4. Colonization (suggested by some council members) was considered by the plantation owners as a long-term process, and thus for the present could not replace the penal sanction.

Salim and his friends lost out on their plea for repeal of the penal code. In the thirties the penal sanction was abolished, in particular, after the United States (the largest importer of plantation rubber) enacted legislation prohibiting entry of goods acquired with indentured labor.

Coolie Legislation and the Penal Sanction on Sumatra's East Coast[2]

Mr. Chairman! Referring to the subject under consideration, even though it fills me with aversion, I cannot say I am disappointed or disillusioned. Expectation or hope for a different outcome should have preceded this sentiment. With me this was not the case. I have learned from experience acquired through plans of the Revision Commission,[3] its memory be blessed, and the government's triumph with the proposal for revision on the political structure of Mr. de Graaff that one can ill rely on the government's promises and explanations. . . .[4]

Mr. President! I am not hopeful, and I have no illusion of the possible success of my opposition against the subject under discussion. Nonetheless I cannot refrain from explaining, in this council, the problem as I perceive it.

First of all, I want to discuss the argument that with this proposition one does not intend to serve capitalist interests, but explicitly has in mind the general interest.

The argument is that the prosperity of the plantations,[5] protected by the penal sanction, is in the general interest of state and society because of the important share in carrying the tax burden and the important contribution in creating this prosperity. Its continued survival [the plantation system] must thus be assured. It is, therefore, necessary that one accords the suppliers of capital guarantees to operate their enterprise and the opportunity to make a profit which will satisfy them and in such a way that they will not prefer to invest their capital elsewhere.

But Mr. Chairman, if the government of this country thinks this way, why should governments of other countries by guided by other considerations? A direct result of this train of thought is naturally a rivalry among the various governments to compete with one another for guarantees of operational security and profit opportunities. Competition, . . . can only be curtailed by the development of the power of the labor unions in each of the countries.

The government takes this into account, has to take this into account.

But what is its attitude toward the other party in the production process: the laborer? I believe, Mr. President, that because the result concerns the general interest, both parties are involved in this. And nonparticipation by one of the parties—regardless which one—threatens economic disruption of society, which Article 161 wants to guard against.

Why then can inadequate profitability—*in casu* wages—and inadequate security of subsistence of the other party, not be ample ground for the abstension of its part, labor, in the production process?

Mr. Chairman! I fully realize that I see here only the theoretical part of the problem, which for the present has no effect on operations. The government does not force the laborer. No, Mr. Chairman. Definitely not. But it also avoids involvement in unemployment, poverty, and the needs of a broad segment of the people and ensures that the fear of—if not actual—hunger and want remains the determinant factor, more than sufficient for the proletarians to continue placing themselves at the disposal of the employers, no matter how miserable, how humiliating, how deadening to their self-esteem the labor conditions may be. And if only the government stopped at that and maintained the principle of laissez faire. But no, Mr. Chairman. This would involve a sympathizing attitude toward the recruitment campaign and the development of labor organizations and actions, adjusting the country's legislation to the historically grown relationships within the economic society. An assurance of the rights acquired by the party of labor in its struggle with capital, which can be done without renouncing the duty of guarding against actual disruption of law and order, against actual assault on person and property.

Under these conditions the government would merit the respect of the whole population, if it would place itself above the parties. But the reality is different.

The government is only capable, I repeat only capable of counting with numbers, with quantities, here and elsewhere, now and in the past, in fact, ever since materialism has dominated the world. With the number of guilders on the one hand and the number of people who are involved in the production process on the other. And the attraction exerted on the government by the long rows of numbers representing guilders, the yield of which offers the prospect of increasing the government's power, is commensurate with the aversion elicited by the possible or actual mobilization of the number of proletarians, conjuring up the possibility of loss of power of this government.

At present this is reality, by the government called its policy. Thus it identifies its interests with the capitalist [interests] of the employers. And puts its power and administration at the disposal—must put at the disposal—of this capitalist group to insure its continued power position. . . . It is by adopting the policy that economic reform or restructuring society cannot occur along the lines of gradual evolution, that revolutionary clashes of opinion become inevitable. To the detriment of humanity in all countries now and in the future. In conflict with the general interest in every country and the whole world.

But Mr. Chairman, it would not be the first time that the party in power confronted with this depiction shrugs its shoulders and thinks *après nous le déluge,* also convinced that its successor in the position of power, if worthy of that position, will keep the party of labor subjugated and oppressed.

Yet the question remains: is it really necessary to maintain even now this blot on our civilization, this slap in the face of humanity?

At the time the penal sanction was established the economic situation of the little man was such that he had food as long as the villagers had food and lodging as long as there were villages. No inescapable need for existence could bind him to his labor, except the labor in his own fields. At that time nearly all labor the little man performed was forced labor with the threat of punishment for those who shirked away from it. This force was a practical necessity, for outside influences involved the population (before their own development and growth compelled them) in a new exotic way of production to meet the needs of a society beyond their own, which as yet had no contact with his [society]. The universality of forced labor at that time did not place the position of the contract coolie on a significantly lower level both in its own as well as in other people's evaluation, and thus did not necessarily exert a depressing influence on his morality.

Now this has changed. This isolation is now ended. Now the struggle for survival has made its entry here too. Now here too unemployment gradually becomes identical with want, lack of housing, and hunger. Now here too the struggle for existence has become like a chain, tying the worker to his labor. The exceptional position requiring exceptional measures no longer exists. There is not yet a new situation in which a militant organization of the proletariat could force a capitalist government to reintroduce exceptional measures. Such measures—and the penal sanction should certainly be considered among these—are both antiquated and premature. And as with other measures having this drawback it can only be—directly or indirectly—detrimental to the desired aim.

The greatest disadvantage of the system must be considered the condition of slavery of the contract coolie for the duration of the contract, a slavery which creates a situation and relationship such as existed during the worst days of slave exploitation, familiar to us from the history of American cotton cultivation which we find described with so much compassion in *Uncle Tom's Cabin*.

Before proceeding with the subject I am taking the liberty to embark on a detour. As a possible although not serious argument for the justification of the penal sanction, I have at one time heard the remark that *adat* and Islam permit and sanction slavery. This argument has not been advanced yet in a public exchange of views. But Mr. Chairman, Islam was done the greatest harm by divulging wrong opinions and presentations because these cannot be easily checked. In particular—as propriety demands—one does not discuss these with people who might be offended, *in casu* the serious believers. In particular those who could rectify the wrong opinion or ideas or in any case will not leave these unrefuted. The result is that the distorted view, called up by partial or total ignorance, is and will remain for many true-to-life.

I am therefore taking the liberty to advance that the form of slavery known to Islam does not in any way resemble the slavery of Uncle Tom and his companions in distress, not even that of the contract coolies under the protection of coolie ordinance and labor inspections, as everyone who takes the trouble to check will be able to verify.

How much better the lot of slaves in Islamic countries is may be inferred from some citations from Snouck's *Mekka:*

> The thousands of Negroes and Abyssinians, who have been abducted to Moslem countries and who still remember their former lives consider that, through slavery, they have become human beings, they are all satisfied and no one is homesick for his country.[6]

As you can see, Mr. Chairman, this description from experience justifies completely my rejection of every comparison between slavery in Islam and that which the world under western domination has witnessed. Naturally one can attribute that to the fact that the economic development in not even one Moslem country has led to the exploitation of the laborer—free or slave. But I would like to point out that the law, the written immutable of the Koran and Hadith, thus apart from the changing economic relationships and conditions, has specified within Islam a legal status for the slave.

As a fine for many transgressions of the rules, the law prescribes compulsory liberation—or redemption—of slaves. Part of the *zakat* is intended for the financial support of slaves who want to buy their freedom and who, on their own initiative, have started this payment in installments.

And as for ethics, for what is considered appropriate to Allah and recommended by the Prophet, I point to the pronouncement of the Prophet:

> Give your servant to eat of the food you eat, clothe him in the clothes that you wear. And if your heart is unwilling to do so, then let him go so that no injustice from you will befall him.

Mr. Chairman! Islam, in particular, is totally unsuitable for justifying the kind of slavery the west knows or, in many respects, the similar position of the contract coolie. . . .

It has been stated that Islam knows and recognizes slavery. As far as I know there is no religion that does otherwise, faced with this phenomenon which indicates merely a stage in the road of the evolution of mankind. A religion would miss its purpose if it did other than provide man with guidelines and courses of actions to regulate his relationship with his environment, his fellowmen and nature, and rules for his own benefit and purification, so that he will be ready, in cooperation with his fellowmen, to steer the development of human society toward ever greater perfection, along lines which the revealed orders and commands have set for men.

. . . thus Islam does not differ from other religions. I only believe I can demand for Islam the recognition that it is the first and only religion which has created a legal status for the slave and has provided ways for his liberation with binding requirements.

Returning to my subject, I must maintain that the relationship between the contract coolie and his employers during the duration of the contract is not different from that of the slave and his master and the overseers at the time of *Uncle Tom's Cabin*. And similar relationships lead to similar and comparable actions. The truth of this is clearly demonstrated by facts made known by the late Mr. van den Brands' publications and the number of isolated cases which, even after the introduction of the coolie ordinance and labor inspection, are occasionally revealed. Weren't some cases quite similar to those in *Uncle Tom's Cabin* that were committed by Legree and his accomplices against the slaves? And yet, Mr. Chairman, Legree or rather his kind date back as far as several decades. And that means a great deal in our world, where even in maltreatment, maiming, and destruction of fellowmen modern methods produce ever more civilized methods.

In the olden days, for instance, one beat the enemy's flesh to pulp with bludgeons and hatchets, splintered his bones and bashed his brains. The beaten enemy was left lying like a heap of dripping dirt. Later, the pellets and hail of the Middle Ages tore the people apart. The lead bullets and dum-dums of the past century beat horrible holes in the human body. Now compare these with the newer methods. The modern weapons make only—excuse this word—flawless corpses.

If we still hear of being flogged or kicked to death, no one could maintain that there exists a real difference between the conscience of the perpetrators and sufferers of these acts and the conscience of slaveowners and overseers and their victims.

Mr. Chairman! We still live in a period, in particular in a colonial country where, and I quote Victor Hugo, "qu'un chat ne s'appelle plus un chat et que Baroche ne s'appelle plus un fripon."[7]

Society and the education geared to it has inculcated in us a bourgeois mentality of propriety in which silence, abuse, and wrongdoings can circumlocute this mentality with justifications, if we cannot furnish clear and, by others, verifiable proof.

Society then stigmatizes us with the name slanderer, and its legal system prosecutes and penalizes us or at best calls our charges insinuations. If only all forces in our society and government could cooperate, we might be able to fight the many wrongs of which we are only too well aware.

However, some truths can no longer be denied. Among these certainly is the maxim that a man's living conditions, his relationship to his environment, have a positive bearing on his psyche and thus on his character. In religion this is recognized in the daily prayer of Christians that God not lead them into temptation and of the Islamites that God not lead them on the road of those who have incurred his wrath and those who were led astray.

I shall not endeavor to undertake an extensive discussion on the character which is formed, or is likely to develop, of the employer and his accomplices, equipped with such extensive powers, guaranteed under the penal sanction, over their subordinates. He who does not ignore the result of scholarly research on the matter cannot deny the dangers of the arrogance and insanity of power which have a dehumanizing influence even on the most good-natured personalities. If the development of this kind of mentality is not curtailed then neither now nor future coolie ordinance and labor inspections will sufficiently counteract manifestations and the results of this frame of mind, which I hope to outline later.

What is the influence of this relationship on the other party: the coolie?

For this party the circumstances have changed considerably, as I stated previously. In former days the aspect of force of the tie binding them did not necessarily have a debasing influence on the coolie. Because at the time forced labor was quite common. In former days even submissiveness was easier to cope with, for then meekness was still a general characteristic of our native people, and no instances of the embittered existed. One cannot deny that this has fundamentally changed. The realization of the debasement through forced labor has penetrated to the lowest level of the population. And after some reflection no one could deny that subjugation and intimidation can no longer evoke permanent slavery, but in the end will bring about a spirit of revolt. How many countries in Europe, now and throughout history, have provided examples of this? How many isolated cases, here, too, are beginning to give the common man understanding and awareness? One can deny or bemoan it, according to one's disposition, but one cannot deny it. . . .

Mr.Chairman, but this cannot be the only result. The dehumanization affects the character of both parties, even beyond the area of mutual contact, thus also their own lives, their own circle. A degeneration of morality, a debasement of men will be the irrefutable consequence. Irrefutable also will be the debasement of all of society, where such relationships involving thousands of people may remain and persist.

Mr. Chairman! Other speakers have already indicated the improvement in attitude which has lately been apparent. Allow me to point out that the fight against the penal sanction and finally the near-certainty of its abolition have contributed a great deal to this.

The bill under discussion, if it is accepted, will bring this fight to a conclusion and frustrate the certainty of its [the Penal Sanction's] abolition forever with the inevitable result: the negation of its corrective action.

Another justification of the penal sanction was advanced . . . that the agreements were voluntarily reached. My esteemed fellow member Stokvis, with whose speech I, incidentally, completely concur, has already scrutinized this free-will argument by citing the testimonies of witnesses that cannot be discounted. My esteemed fellow member Kerkkamp did likewise. I need not add anything to it. But permit me, Mr. Chairman to ask the attention of our council for a comparison.

I am sure one will recall the intervention of a former resident of the Lampong districts in the social and economic life of his subjects by the ordered abolition of the *bini-dapur* system.[8] Covert slavery one said. The *bini-dapur* is exploited by performing work in the pepper plantations. In the home of her master she has only a little room next to the kitchen. It takes little to provide for her; she is treated as an inferior.

Mr. Chairman! In general, one has approved or at least not condemned the intervention by the resident, and yet no one could maintain that the lot of the *bini-dapur* was worse than that of a contract coolie.

It cannot be denied, in particular not by those who refer to the stated voluntariness of the contract agreement, that a Moslem marriage, even with a *bini-dapur,* presumes the consent of the woman, if she is an adult, thus a voluntary contract agreement. And then one must concede that the *bini-dapur,* especially when she bears children, must partake in the inheritance of her master and husband.

Mr. Chairman! These are only a few points which merit consideration. In particular for those who did not have any objections against the intervention of the former resident, it should be evident that the freedom of action of the *bini-dapur* at contracting the marriage is comparable to that of the indentured contract coolie at the time of the agreement.

Mr. Chairman! To avert watching disapproving faces I shall not continue to speak on the in-fact existing crimping in the hiring of coolies. For even when extortion takes place in the recruitment of *hadjis,* solely because one receives a percentage of the purchase of tickets, money, and premiums of the *hadji*-sjeichs in Mecca, one should not be surprised that in the hiring of coolies (where the premiums often are higher than in the recruitment of *hadjis*) one has to deal with crimping.

Mr. Chairman! In conclusion I cannot say a single word in justification of the existence, and even less of the continuation, of the penal sanction. That I have nonetheless put my signature under the motion of my respected fellow member Stokvis and others,[9] does not mean that I shall be satisfied with the implementation of the conditions mentioned in the motion. But I, too, understand that a great deal of time is needed to clean up dirt, if one does not wish to throw the dirt on another heap, where it can cause as much harm.

NOTES

1. H. G. Heijting, *De Koelie Wetgeving voor de Buitengewesten van Nederlandsch Indie* (The Hague: van Stockum, 1925) pp. 125-187, provides useful background material.
2. From *Djedjak Langkah Hadji Agus Salim* (Djakarta: Tintamas, 1954), pp. 83-96. Original title, "Wijziging en Aanvulling van de Koelie Ordonnantie Sumatra's Oostkust," speech delivered in the People's Council. Dutch East Indies, Volksraad, *Handelingen,* session 1923-1924, November 2, 1923. Translated with permission of the publisher Tintamas and the heirs of H. A. Salim.
3. Salim was a member of the 1920 Revision Commission.
4. Simon de Graaff, Minister of Colonies, who reneged on most of the promises of sweeping reform made to the Indonesians by Governor-General van Limburg Stirum in 1918.
5. In Dutch the word *cultures* was used meaning the cultivation of marketable crops on a large scale, for example, the plantations.
6. Salim here quotes extensively (about a page and a half) from Snouck's *Mekka,* written in German, of which I have translated one paragraph. Snouck describes the lot of the slaves (which is apparently far from unpleasant) and concludes that

7. the treatment accorded slaves in some of the Moslem countries of the Middle East is better than the treatment of slaves in Uncle Tom's days.

8. Literally, that a cat is no longer called a cat and that Baroche (a high-ranking official under Napoleon III) is no longer called a crook. Victor Hugo was a French writer who for many years was exiled from France.

8. Resident, third rank from the bottom, in the Dutch administrative hierarchy. He was head of a residency.

   Lampong is an area in South Sumatra, which has extensive pepper plantations.

9. J. E. Stokvis had introduced a motion to have the government, rather than private industry, participate in the production process. The motion never came to a vote.

Mohammad Husni Thamrin: Pragmatic Politician (1894-1941)

Those who have the time and fortitude to peruse the People's Council debates from 1927 through 1940 will be able to observe, with considerable pleasure, the development and growth of a remarkable and ambitious man, Mohammad Husni Thamrin.[1] Boldly and courageously he advocated the nationalist cause from the council floor. Called "outstanding" by one governor-general and "dangerous and smart" by another,[2] Thamrin never failed to utilize an opportunity to expose the inequities of colonialism and the speciousness of the much-lauded Dutch sense of justice.

The son of a public proscecutor,[3] he was born on February 16, 1894 in Batavia, where he attended Dutch public and private schools, and was graduated from the King William III High School. After a brief stint as a writer in a government administrative office he secured a position in the bookkeeping department of the Indies' largest interisland shipping company, where he remained employed for ten years.

His political career commenced when he was appointed to the Batavia municipal council at the age of twenty-five. In 1925 he was elected by the members, from among their membership, to serve as one of their four aldermen, the first Indonesian to fill this position. In 1929 he became second deputy-mayor and shortly thereafter mayor pro tempore of the Batavia municipality.

His activities in the municipal council brought him to the attention of Governor-General de Graeff, who greatly admired him and appointed him to the People's Council in 1927 when Dr. Sutomo who was offered the seat first, declined. Thamrin was reappointed in 1931, elected in 1935, and reelected in 1939.

M. H. Thamrin

Thamrin's career as leader of the nationalist movement in the council was established with the formation of the Fraksi Nasional in 1930. In the following decade he made many attempts to improve the lot of his countrymen, although many of his proposals were either rejected or withdrawn. He submitted a motion to abrogate the governor-general's power to exile, without trial, the politically dangerous; to abolish Boven Digul, the deportation colony; he advocated the formation of an Indonesian militia; urged for an investigation of labor conditions on plantations; he called for the use of the Indonesian language in all the councils in the archipelago; and for the official use of the words Indonesia and Indonesian.

At the outset of his career, cooperation appeared to Thamrin to be a valid means of securing political concessions. Yet he was not a minion and rather deftly utilized the cloak of parliamentary immunity and thus speedily became to conservative Dutchmen the most hated and feared Indonesian of the thirties. Thamrin realized that cooperation provided courses of action apparently not sufficiently investigated by Sukarno, and scornfully rejected by M. Hatta and S. Sjahrir, all of whom were banished in 1934 and rendered ineffective.

Thamrin's efforts to bring about change were not confined to the People's Council, he also played an active role in the various political organizations. In the late twenties he became chairman of Kaum Betawi, a party seeking to advance the interests of the Indonesian population of the capital city; in the thirties he joined Parindra, a political coalition aimed at elevating the status of the Indonesian people, with the ultimate goal of securing independence. After the defeat of the Sutardjo Petition in 1938, Thamrin initiated the GAPI movement,[4] a federation of parties seeking more independence from the Netherlands; and in 1939 he launched the drive for an Indonesian parliament.

On January 6, 1941 Thamrin was confined to house arrest, and his home was searched. The purported reason for this unprecedented action was a personal letter that he had sent to the journalist Tabrani in May 1940, making highly derogatory remarks about the Dutch government-in-exile in London. Tabrani and Thamrin, once close friends, had quarreled and the former had published Thamrin's letter. For some time prior to the arrest, rumors were rife that Thamrin, a very astute and successful merchant, had engaged in more than business relations with the Japanese.[5] But to many Indonesians the arrest of the popular vice-chairman of the People's Council was seen as an attempt to discredit him.

Thamrin died of a heart attack five days after his arrest, obviating the need for the colonial government to furnish a plausible explanation. Allusions that Thamrin was a traitor and an Indonesian Wang Ching-wei were without foundation. To many of Indonesia's leaders, the status as a nation subjugated by a western power had become untenable. Years of dealing with the colonial government had taught Thamrin that the Dutch would never relinquish power voluntarily. Exasperation with his futile efforts to secure even minor concessions may well have led him to seek Japan's intercession.[6] But his goal was and remained Indonesian independence.[7]

NOTES

1. Much of the data used in this sketch has been derived from the following sources: Tamar Djaja, *Pusaka Indonesia Orang-Orang Besar Tanah Air* (Bandung: Kolff, n.d.), pp. 180-186; Matu Mona, *Riwayat Penghidupan dan Perdjuangan Moh. Husni Thamrin* (Medan: Pustaka Timur, 1950); D. M. G. Koch, *Batig Slot. Figuren uit het oude Indie* (Amsterdam: De Brug-Djambatan, 1960), pp. 154-162.

2. S. L. van de Wal, *De Volksraad en de Staatkundige Ontwikkeling van Nederlands-Indie II* (Groningen: Wolters, 1965), p. 42. The statement was made by Governor-General de Graeff.

    Statement of Governor-General de Jonghe, who considered Thamrin smart and dangerous and even more dangerous because he could not be caught. D M. G. Koch, *Om de Vrijheid* (Djakarta: Jajasan Pembangunan, 1950), p. 115.

3. Thamrin Mohammad Thabri was adjunct *hoofddjaksa* of the *landraad* in Batavia since 1894. *Regeeringsalmanak voor Nederlandsch Indie II, 1903* (Batavia: Landsdrukkerij, 1903), p. 72.

4. Van de Wal, *De Volksraad,* pp. 406-408, mentions a meeting on GAPI (*Ga*bungan *P*olitik *I*ndonesia) between Thamrin and the government spokesman for General Affairs, who advanced objections concerning the first paragraph of the federation's manifest, which stated that the danger threatening the authorities of the Netherlands Indies and Indonesian society was increasing daily.

5. J. de Kadt, *Indonesische Tragedie* (Amsterdam: van Oorschot, 1949), pp. 49-50.

6. Van de Wal, *De Volksraad,* pp. 587-592, cites a letter, dated November 28, 1940, of an Indonesian lawyer to the Solicitor General, accusing Thamrin of conspiring with the Japanese commercial delegation that visited Indonesia in September 1940. Allegedly Thamrin and the Japanese had made plans on how to govern Indonesia after a new order in Southeast Asia was established by Japan. Although the letter may be indicative of the sentiment that some felt about Thamrin's power position, it cannot be taken as proof that he actually made such plans.

7. *Overzicht van de Inlandse en Maleis-Chinese Pers* (Weltevreden: Bureau voor de Volkslectuur, 1938), p. 365. Article by M. H. Thamrin in *Pemandangan,* May 18, 1938.

Editor's Introduction:
A Nationalist Party in the People's Council

On December 29, 1929 Sukarno and other members of the Partai Nasional Indonesia were arrested and widespread house searches were conducted over the archipelago. The motive for this police action was purportedly the imminent seizure of power by the PNI and Sukarno. No evidence to this effect was ever found.

The establishment of the Nationalist Faction *(Fraksi Nasional)* was not only in reply to the arrests and searches but was also intended as a counterforce to the newly founded ultrareactionary Dutch organization, the Fatherland Club, which envisaged preserving Dutch power in the archipelago indefinitely.

Announcing the Formation of the Nationalist Faction[1]

Mr. Chairman! Like my predecessor on the rostrum,[2] I would like to notify you of the formation of a new faction which, indeed, is not that big that its membership amounts to several thousands like the faction of the former speaker, but which has as its guideline that quality is more important than quantity to wit the formation of a nationalist faction,[3] for the time being, consisting of ten members of the People's Council. Its program is as follows:

Article I. The nationalist faction of the People's Council has as its goal to accomplish Indonesian autonomy as rapidly as possible.

Article II. It tries to implement this objective:
   a. by working for political reform
   b. by working for the abolition of all political, economic, and intellectual differences which result from the colonial antithesis
   c. by employing all legal means

The following members have joined this faction, namely, Messrs. Kusumo Utoyo, Dwidjosewojo, Datuk Kajo, Mochtar, Nja Arif, Soangkupon, Pangeran Ali, Sutadi, Suroso, and Thamrin. The last one was appointed chairman.

Mr. Chairman! Proceeding with the general discussion I would—if I occupied a position comparable to that of the Government Spokesman for General Affairs, but then of course of the organized nationalist movement—give a speech which, in intent, structure, and choice of words could be copied verbatim from the address of last January 10 by the esteemed Government Spokesman of General Affairs.

If I were occupying such a position the speech would have sounded as follows:

Mr. Chairman, we have instantly considered it our duty to assert our position as members of the People's Council;[4] we regard the recently conducted house searches manifestations of overt distrust toward the nationalist movement in general and the PNI in particular. We have considered whether it might not be better, mindful of the advice suggested by the magazine *Timbul,* to refrain from exchanging views with the government in this matter, for silence could be eloquent proof of the feeling of unrest, and in many people of bitterness, well-nigh throughout the entire native movement because of the house searches of leaders and nonleaders of the PNI and an even greater number of nonleaders and nonmembers of the PNI.

Mr. Chairman! Naturally we are aware that the People's Council could, and some members would, demand an explanation, but aside from that an account from us might be necessary and useful to eliminate possible misconceptions and misunderstandings. The wish of the College of Delegates to be informed without delay,[5] expressed in the motion of Messrs. Kusumo Utoyo and others and accepted without a roll call,[6] has merely confirmed our assumption in this respect.

This, as you can see, Mr. Chairman, is nearly a verbatim copy of the address of the government spokesman. The following sentences will also be a nearly verbatim rendition. In the following statement I shall first explain, concentrating on the main issues, what considerations have motivated our attitude. Subsequently I would like to devote a word to the announcement of the temporary effects. Finally, I propose to consider briefly the current situation as far as present and future administrative policy is concerned.

Mr. Chairman, what engendered these feelings of unrest and bitterness? To answer this question I would like to recall how we, already in our action of 1926, warned against eliciting favorable expectation prematurely, how these warnings were repeated during the previous session of the People's Council for the umpteenth time in the following words:

> Although the data, submitted by both sides justifying their positions, does not offer anything positive that one can discern as *Leitmotiv* of the section report, as far as the political part is concerned, there is a feeling of discomfort by those groups who a few years ago directed their hopes with great confidence toward the newly inaugurated administration of the Governor-General.
>
> Yet, Mr. Chairman, although my political objections have in many respects been satisfied by the official government explanation, I cannot

refrain from mentioning that the political phase inaugurated this year appears to demonstrate why feelings are running high, because now the atmosphere is cleared as far as communism is concerned, attention is demanded for "second-degree troublemakers," with the probable intention to mop them up as well, although not directly by internment, at least socially and spiritually.

The impression indeed has been evoked that by emphasizing the dangerous aspect of the extreme nationalist effort, one will pave the way for further measures against groups which do not directly and unconditionally conform to government policy, as if the government is cautiously trying to assess correctly the political feeling of the masses.

Thus sounded the expressions of worry, Mr. Chairman! If this assumption is proved to be true, then only deeds would follow. This would indeed have taken place, if the nationalist movement had been in a position where it could have taken action . . . but now only can stammer words where deeds might be more appropriate. Since mid-July, when the words cited by me were spoken, followed by the so-called last warning of the Government Spokesman for General Affairs last August—a warning which cannot be a warning because of the vague formulation and ambiguous phraseology leaving room for all kinds of interpretation—the principal leaders, in particular of the PNI, mindful of the experience of others and, because of the colonial administration, overcautious in their actions as well as in their pronouncements, these PNI leaders have indeed urged their followers not to tread the path of violence and to conduct the struggle to accomplish the goals of their organization only through legal means.

Others, invariably persons without a position of responsibility in the movement, have in lectures or public meetings urged those present, in crystal clear language, to be calm. And, to obey orders, even though the authorities appeared unjust and unreasonable.

Notwithstanding the anxiety of some ambitious servants of the administration, these statements could not possibly be considered to exceed the legal limits. Legal authority was never disparaged in these admonitions. The servant of the authorities, who sometimes wanted to venture on illegal paths, was courteously reminded that everyone, even the most important and highest servants, should submit to the enacted laws; thus listeners could never have received the impression that the end of this authority was at hand. And no feelings of dissatisfaction and fantastic expectations could have been evoked, not even in central Preangan. Therefore in the long run no tension could have developed, not even by a further increase of the influence of the nationalist movement. Therefore, an eruption of violence could never have occurred, although it would have been welcomed by the ambitious and injudicious as an inducement "to trounce them [the nationlists] soundly."

Whereas the nationalist movement was now debating how, on the one hand, the auspicious situation could be tempered (for its influence was visibly and perceptibly increasing), while on the other hand, this state of affairs was a matter of concern, for this increase constituted the greatest danger to its existence. During all of last year several indications and reports on the impending threat of intervention by those in power came from various sources. Rumors arose throughout the year, sporadically and without specific substance or connection. Thus in the past year more than once, one heard of the possibility of an intervention in 1929 or 1930. Without underestimating them, such rumors must be tested for their true merit. Regardless of the reports heard about the imminent intervention by the government, regardless of the many admonitions and warnings of people (considered by the leaders as overcautious and enervated sufferers who see ghosts by day), regardless of the conviction among the leaders that, in a colonial society extreme caution was to be observed, regardless of the peaceful purpose, Mr. Chairman, regardless of the reports (at times exceeding fifty),[7] faith in the righteousness of their cause finally prevailed—faith in the sense of justice of those who guard over law and order, faith in the purity of the intentions of the nationalist movement, the conviction that they had complete control over the situation, the knowledge that their actions were absolutely within the limits of the law, and the belief that the principles espoused by the government would be adhered to.

Each symptom of an extreme position by every member was strictly watched, the selection of members was safeguarded by guarantees, so that, humanly speaking, mistakes, although not excluded, were reduced to a minimum.

Delusions of various attractions as freedom from paying taxes, brick houses, cash money, and so on if one joined the movement was not used as a means of enlarging influence and was completely rejected by the leadership of the nationalist movement in general and the PNI in particular, because they are above such a pedestrian manner of expanding their power. Pressure and intimidation are unknown to their purpose.

On the contrary, at nearly every meeting or assembly Ir. Sukarno reminded the people of the Garibaldi's words to his followers when they asked what the reward for their adherence would be. And the answer invariably was: hunger, misery, rags, and troubles will be yours.

Under the circumstances mentioned here, Mr. Chairman, it is understandable that all the principal leaders of the PNI and other organizations left their posts and went to Solo, where other duties called them. It would simply have been irresponsible, Mr. Chairman, if they had left their posts when they expected a serious event to take place, which could have led to a clash, no matter how small (for on such occasions the population always suffers most). . . .

Therefore there was no cause for a judicial, political intervention, yes, not even based on the suspicion that a misdemeanor might take place. The provisional application of Article 108 of the Penal Code, the conspiracy to revolt, as well of Article 169, the participation in an association which plans the commitment of a misdemeanor, does not surprise us in the least. To elaborate allow me to refer to the case of Mr. Kusuma Sumantri on which the government's memo states:

> A proposal to intern Mr. Kusuma Sumantri will reach the government soon. Further information on this will be furnished in due course.

This declaration to employ political measures should be compared with the statement in the *Handelingen* of only a few months ago when the government emphatically stated:

> I cannot give you any information because the investigation is still pending before the judge. I can, however, at the request of Mr. Thamrin, supply some indication on the articles on which Mr. Kusuma Sumantri's detention was based. They are articles 88 jo and 108 concerning conspiracy against the legal government and 109 dealing with incitement to revolt.

I hope, Mr. Chairman, that you and the other gentlemen in this council will understand and realize, by comparing the cited government statements, why a person is proscecuted under the law but not penalized and that political measures are resorted to as a result of the judicial prosecution.

One can observe the same obvious connection between judicial prosecution and employment of political measures regarding the now detained and accused, when Portia, on the basis of existing laws, is forced to withdraw from the performance of her duty.

The government's reply states:

> And such an exchange of views (the exchange of views on the value of the discovered documents and/or reliability of given testimony) would be inadmissible as long as the court is considering whether legal action against one or more PNI leaders can and must be instituted. It will then become the task of the judges to decide this validity, a function the government cannot under any circumstances speculate upon nor exert influence on. However, if because of objections derived from formal testimony, referral to the judge of the pending case cannot take place then either release or internment will follow.

In plain language I conclude, Mr. Chairman, that the government will possibly not abide by a court decision but wants to feel free to resort to such political measures as internment, if the courts it has established (and the formal and informal testimony it supplied) did not mete out to the culprits what the government considers appropriate. I am inclined to call out here, and I hope to see signs of approval: Long live judicial investigation!

The action of the government was, I might say although in keeping with the law, unjust and unnecessary.

We are confident, Mr. Chairman, that the criticism against the government on the latest house searches will be correctly assessed. The government will then admit and recognize that the extent of the house searches and the reasons advanced to justify these were not only irresponsible but even gave the appearance of provocation to incitement.

Chairman: I request Mr. Thamrin, to withdraw the words that the Government committed provocation.[8]

I am using the same words that the Government Spokesman for General Affairs has used, Mr. Chairman.

Regardless of how much pressure was exerted on the government by unbalanced officials as a result of the systematically cultivated-fear-neuroses by the white press, the government had no choice but rather the duty to oppose this forcefully. Duty to consider carefully and cautiously the risk as well as the results of such an action in the event of insufficient evidence or indications. No one would blame the government had it intervened if, indeed, justifiable suspicion of an impending revolt had existed or if proof had been produced to confirm these suspicions.

Because nothing of the sort existed, the government assumed the consequences of an unnecessary and needless provocation of the sense of justice of that particular part of the population. . . . the depiction of the weekly *Het Indische Volk* [The Indies People], namely, [was] that the government appeared to have been pressured by rightist elements—perhaps possibly under pretext of a smoldering plot—which carried the government along.

Mr. Chairman, aside from the veracity contained in this depiction, the government action against the PNI is termed political. But, *mirabile dictum,* this description happens to be correct and can only be useful and serve to clarify an exchange of thoughts.

Actions against the previously mentioned organizations were actually unnecessary to protect society in its entirety or in part against attack. Mr. Chairman, if the action of the house searches was not justified as far as the results it produced, the government, for the present, may have to curtail giving information, because, contrary to expectations, the house searches have rendered nothing tangible.

For, apart from this, despite the highly increased activity between December 29 and now, government has not succeeded irrefutably to prove the formal accusation with documents and reliable written accounts, despite the intensive and large-scale house searches. . . .

I do not have to elaborate, Mr. Chairman, that if we can provide the council, in due course, with further information we shall not refrain from doing this but we shall keep this body informed, as always.

Finally, Mr. President, a few words on the current situation. First, I would like to draw attention to the performance of the administration and the police, in particular, the detective service, which accomplished frightening the community on a grand scale (although the proper operation and implementation of given instructions is obvious in a well-organized administration). Thus the "by-the-government-ordered" intervention could not yield, contrary to expectation, the results the government had expected. . . . The nationalist movement has entrusted me to protest against these large-scale house searches. . . . The nationalist movement also protests strongly the fact that, apparently in some places, the regent was prevented from participating as he should have in the preparation and execution of emergency measures.

The government must have anticipated, in view of the scope of the action . . . and been aware of the feelings of the majority of administrative officials toward the nationalist movement in general and the PNI in particular, the government, . . . in view of the scope and the little time available, should have foreseen and anticipated what would have been the result of exceeding the limits set by the Attorney General.

Mr. Chairman, the instruction concerned exclusively an investigation of the homes and offices of the leaders of the PNI and their persons as well as likely places where secret warehouses, partly or completely, would be in use by this organization. Mr. Chairman, nothing in this order could have prompted the scope of the house searches or the arrest of persons not members of the PNI or of buildings not used or partly used by the PNI.

Therefore, Mr. Chairman, it is obvious why people who had no relationship with the PNI were searched and interrogated and why buildings were searched, where, despite all efforts no PNI contact could be assumed. In view of the instructions it is also apparent and clear that exceeding the stated limits was not confined to a single place, but that everywhere exactly the same event took place. In every place where house searches were conducted, everyone was systematically examined, homes of those who had but a tenuous connection with the native movement were searched . . . such as [members of] Pasundan, Budi Utomo, Sarekat Sumatra, . . . Taman Siswo, and the Persatuan Cooperatie Indonesia, and Muhammadijah. We emphatically declare that we are unable to explain the cleverness of the people charged with the implementation; there must have existed a telepathic contact between the commissioner, who did not intend to search person and home of non-PNI members, and those who carried out orders and also did not intend to conduct searches of homes of non-PNI members, but who nonetheless did. We live and learn, Mr. Chairman.

Such action, although not intended, was widespread. Mr. Chairman, one example. At the Muhammadijah School in Kemajoran, according to a board member of that organization, the police entered the building. Why? Because in this building education is provided, because there are desks, because one teacher is a member of Pasundan and another of the Sarekat Sumatra, and because these teachers have had, from time to time, meetings with some PNI members with whom they are acquainted. Although one of the teachers lived in the building, the police did not deem necessary to alert him. They simply surrounded the building, preventing the children from entering, then proceeded to break open bookcases containing the children's text and reading books. Another group searched the bathroom and storage room, as well as the suitcases of two visiting lady teachers, who, because of the PPI convention—a women's convention—Mr. Chairman! were guests of one of the lady teachers of the Muhammadijah School.

It was even considered necessary to lift up the sarong of one of the custodians to see if perchance the so eagerly sought documents and revolt plans were hidden there. Such searches by non-PNI members can be supplemented by countless others ad libitum, such as those that have taken place of members of Pasundan, Sarekat Sumatra, Budi Utomo, members of the municipal council, teachers of the People's University, officials of the *mantri* police, a *djaksa* member of the native court, a former district head in Sumatra's East Coast, in editorial offices in Bandjarmassin Sumatra's East Coast and in Garut.

To summarize: Batavia 50 house searches, Bandung 41, Cheribon 24, Pekalongan 42, Sukabumi and Tjandjur 31, Solo 11, Kudus 6, Djokja 35, Padang 2, Medan 25, Semarang 30, Tebing Tinggi unknown, Pangkalan Brandan 12, Krawang 25, Serang everyone engaged in politics, Garut 20, Malang unknown, Blitar unknown, Palembang unknown, Gresik 6, Buitenzorg 20, Surabaya about 20, Telok Betong unknown, Bandjarmassin 5 (see *Suluh Rajat Indonesia* no. 1, January 1, 1930), Lubukpakam and Galand at 2 *Budi Utomo* schools, Tandjung Balei several . . . Siantar 8, Macassar 28, Bindjei 5, and in the environs 3 (see *Bataviaas Niewsblad,* 31 December 1929).

Action, such as described, in view of the given instructions, was wrong and inappropriate. Therefore it is unquestionable, Mr. Chairman, that the government policy toward the nationalist movement—I am authorized to emphasize this—has remained unchanged. If that policy has remained unchanged then what has happened is the confused result of that policy. The existence within the present movement of a division between evolutionaries and revolutionaries, between socially constructive labor, on the one hand, and socially destructive action, on the other, was always denied.[9]

The movement has always emphasized the important obligation to safeguard the essence of the normal development of the indigenous society against police brutality and weapons. Nonetheless the nationalist movement will continue, peacefully and unobtrusively, aware of what needs to be done. All hope of annihilation, even of serious paralysis, will prove in vain.

To date the government has not explained the exact distinction between what can be encouraged as socially productive and/or permissible and what is socially destructive and must be attacked and destroyed. The result of the government's ever-changing principles has accomplished that those parts of the PNI which have exceeded the operational limits set by the government will be destroyed. What standards determine these limits is so very nicely not stated or is put in such ambivalent phrases and terms that at all times the government can safely refer to these. . . .

I would like to summarize the statement just given on the nationalist movement by noting the presence of a feeling of complete dissatisfaction with the government's explanation; rather than acts of justice the organized house searches and its results were deeds of political reaction and curtailment of the right of assembly and of arbitrary power.

Mr. Chairman. I would have spoken at least in this way, had I been the representative of the proscribed Indonesian nationalist movement, but as I am not in this position, I, as a lowly subject, stammer (used to swallow a great deal and to accept as logical everything supposed to be): Alhamdulillah, Praise the Lord! May the Lord's blessing rest on this attitude as well.

Thank you, Mr. Chairman.

NOTES

1. Speech delivered in the People's Council, January 27, 1930. *Handelingen* (1929-1930):1646-1651.

2. Referring to a speech made by R. Fruin, member of the conservative Dutch group, the Fatherland Club.
3. In an article in *Jubileum Nummer Perhimpoenan Indonesia* (Leiden, n.p., 1938), Thamrin explained that the name *Nationale Fractie* [Nationalist faction] was a misnomer, because *fractie* is a group of members belonging to a political party, who work together within a representative body. Members of the Nationalist Faction belonged to different parties and some were nonparty members. Besides the People's Council was not a representative body.
4. The People's Council had limited powers. These included: colegislative powers in ordinances pertaining to internal matters of the Indies; the right to give advice; the right of petition, investigation, and questioning. Members of the council also enjoyed parliamentary immunity for what they had said in the council.
5. The Council of Delegates, consisting of thirty members, was a working body within the council and had the same powers and rights. Its members were chosen by the council from among its membership.
6. Motion Kusumo Utoyo (cosigned by Messrs. Roep, Sukawati, Sujono, and de Hoog) requested an explanation because of the feeling of unrest these actions had produced. *Handelingen,* Volksraad, College van Gedelegeerden (1929-1930):80.
7. This statement refers to the continuous predictions in the conservative Dutch press that Sukarno and the PNI were plotting to take over the government.
8. Thamrin did not retract his statement here but had to do so later.
9. See pp. 144-145 (herein) for Mr. Hatta's comments on evolutionaries and revolutionaries.

Editor's Introduction:
The Fate of the Sutardjo Petition

The Sutardjo Petition, named after its first signatory Sutardjo Kartohadikusumo, was introduced in the People's Council on July 15, 1936. It asked for the convocation of an imperial conference to grant Indonesia autonomy within a period of ten years.[1]

The Explanatory Statement indicated that no rupture with the Netherlands was envisioned, on the contrary, the belief was the two parts of the kingdom were economically interdependent. The motivation for the proposed conference was a feeling of hopelessness, which had pervaded the indigenous population as well as its leaders and which was believed to be detrimental to the unity of the kingdom.

In the beginning there appeared to be little interest in the petition from the Indonesian side. However, gradually its significance permeated the ranks of the major nationalist groups, and the day the petition came to a vote the visitors gallery of the People's Council was packed with Indonesians.[2] On September 26, 1936, the council accepted the petition with twenty-six for and twenty against.[3]

When the Dutch parliament appeared slow in acting on the petition a committee was formed to seek support among the Indonesian people. One of the committee members was Hadji Agus Salim.[4]

It took the Dutch parliament more than two years to reject the petition, completely ignoring the sentiments among the Indonesian leaders. Only two votes were cast in favor of the petition: by the Indonesian communist Rustam Effendi and by the socialist Professor Van Gelderen.[5]

The Nationalist Faction and the Sutardjo Petition

Mr. Chairman! Our faction is of the opinion that the Sutardjo proposal as such does not in any way respond to our ideals or to reasonable expectations of other nationalist organizations, which have less far-reaching goals.

All the petition proposition has in common with the constitutional status of dominion is the name. Missing are guidelines on how the proposed goal could be reached. Judging from the speeches of the several signatories there appears to be disagreement on some of the important parts of the petition. Therefore, the program in its entirety cannot entice us.

There is, however, one aspect of the proposition which is regarded somewhat favorably by the great majority of our faction,[6] and that is the request to convene a conference with the Netherlands to discuss the future constitutional status of these lands. This part of our faction wants to promote convening this conference, regardless of the goal and the scope of the petition itself. We would like to note that the present political situation must be changed, and the current political status must be termed untenable.

Thus voting for the petition can only be regarded as a declaration of our willingness to participate in the proposed conference and to assist in the formulation of the, by us considered imperative, change in the political and constitutional status of these lands.

NOTES

1. J. M. Pluvier, *Overzicht van de Ontwikkeling der Nationalistische Beweging in Indonesia* (The Hague: W. van Hoeve, 1953), pp. 118-129.
2. *A. I. D. de Preanger Bode* (Bandung), September 29, 1936, p. 3. This newspaper considered the engagement of the Dutch princess more important and relegated the news of the petition to the third page.
3. Dutch East Indies, Volksraad, *Handelingen,* September 29, 1936.
4. S. L. van de Wal, *De Volksraad,* pp. 236, 285-286.
5. Pluvier, *Overzicht,* p. 126.
6. Four members of the faction voted against. In their opinion the petition did not go far enough.

Editor's Introduction:
Toward Racial Integration

On December 11, 1940, M. H. Thamrin proposed an amendment to the defense budget that would have equalized soldiers' pay, regardless of race.¹

The motion was voted on the next day and, as expected, was defeated with thirteen votes for (all Indonesians) and twenty-three against (including three Indonesians loyal to colonialism).²

The government's argument in opposing equal pay was that there was no money available to raise salaries and a reduction in salaries to secure equalization would result in prompting many European soldiers to leave the service.

Proposal for Equal Pay for Soldiers Regardless of Race[3]

Mr. Chairman. As you have already announced a member of my faction, Lapian, is unable to speak . . . and he has requested that I speak for him. I would like to start by thanking you, Mr. Chairman, for the opportunity granted me to speak for Mr. Lapian, and I do so with pleasure for he pleads for a fair and just cause, namely, the attempt to secure equal pay for all military personnel of equal rank, regardless of race.

Mr. Chairman, this is not a new problem. I recall that since the establishment of the People's Council, Indonesians have advocated equal pay for soldiers. In every People's Council session one or more Indonesians, some more urgently than others, have spoken out against the differentiation of the soldiers' pay.

The struggle for equal pay for soldiers is not exclusively a matter of material gain. Besides considerations of fairness that for equal work and equal risks equal pay should be received, the different and lower pay of the Indonesian soldier contains an element of racial offense, to wit, the implication of racial inferiority.

This is the reason and will remain the reason that the Indonesians will continue to press for abolition of the race criterion in every branch of government service and the elimination of every instance of race discrimination in determining wages. We have now reached the stage in which the race criterion has already been abolished in civil service positions.

The Royal Netherlands Indies Army is still an impregnable fortress—to speak in military terms—in maintaining the race as the principle determinant of soldiers' pay. As this bastion—in the eyes of the Indonesians—like all other racial bastions must be conquered and destroyed, one may expect continued violent attack from us. The preservation of race as the principle in determining wages is for me, and I believe for many Indonesians, unacceptable. Thus we cannot possibly vote in favor of the military budget. As I have said before in every session of the People's Council, Indonesian paladins have pleaded for equal pay for soldiers.

In this session[4] Mr. Lapian distinguished himself in his pleading for equality.

In the struggle of the People's Council against the government—if I may label it this way—for equal pay for all soldiers regardless of race, two prominent features emerge. In the first place it is characteristic that, over the years, the wording of the government's reply has changed and become more cautious. In former years it was readily admitted that the pay was indeed based on the race criterion; the government, despite the differentiated pay, had enough candidates for the soldiers' job; there was no reason to bring about change.

Over the years and with the increase in the awareness of race consciousness of the Indonesians, the language of the government has changed.

Now one no longer says that wages are based on race but (I cite from the government reply of August 1, 1940, *Handelingen* 283), Mr. Chairman, on the "standard of living, what is fair and what is not fair."

These are different words for what is in fact the same problem. One now refers to living needs and conditions and what is fair and not fair. But when such language amounts to more pay and more privileges for the European soldier, this means racial preference and racial discrimination.

Emphasizing the need criterion as the basic point in the argument for unequal soldiers' pay is untenable, because no two persons, European or not, have an identical standard of living. Such a criterion would necessarily entail pay determined on a personal basis for each soldier of the Royal Netherlands Indies Army. Unquestionably the unequal wages are based on racial discrimination between the different population groups, and one cannot argue away the fact with clever and complicated formulae.

Another notable aspect in the fight of the People's Council in pleading for equal pay is that the reply of the government invariably circumvents the basic point and always leaves the main issue unanswered.

From the outset Mr. Lapian took the position that wages must be equal, and to support his arguments he cited several instances demonstrating the inequity of the existing differentiated pay for soldiers.

The result of this method has been that the government based its arguments primarily on adventitious conditions and left the basic points unanswered. This happened previously and happened again this time. Besides, the arguments of the government focused on minor points, and now the government advances in its reply dubious and unworthy reasons. The government states, namely . . .

> Their material position—of the indigenous military personnel in question—is in keeping with all reasonable demands and conforms with that of other government officials of comparable rank. One can safely assume that a feeling of dissatisfaction does not emanate spontaneously from the feelings of the Indigenous soldier, but naturally it is not very difficult to make the simple soldier dissatisfied, when someone explains to him, presenting certain facts, that he actually should be dissatisfied. And therefore the speeches of Messrs. Lapian and Sutardjo are actually a threat to the spirit of the military personnel in question.

Mr. Chairman, the esteemed government spokesman is here suggesting that the Indonesian soldier is basically satisfied with differentiated pay but that he is made to feel more or less dissatisfied by the description of conditions presented by the arguments of Mr. Lapian and Mr. Sutardjo.

I shall not go so far as to register my protest against the here cited statement of the esteemed government spokesman. Suffice it to say that I only wish to register vehement objections against the government's methods and arguments. And besides the opinion of the government spokesman is incorrect when he says that the Indonesian soldier is not of his own volition dissatisfied with the differentiated pay. Even an Indonesian soldier is a human being, and it is very understandable that, when he observes daily the grievous inequitous treatment while performing the same tasks and running the same risks, he himself will make comparisons and will not be satisfied with the given situation.

Another argument of the esteemed government spokesman is that he believes that the spirit among the Indonesian soldiers is good because he has heard so few complaints. This to me is a specious argument, because the discipline in the army is so strict that to voice complaints on differentiated pay is impossible. If the esteemed government spokesman would give soldiers permission to express themselves freely, he would hear different comments.

Mr. Chairman! I find the government's arguments unworthy. I for my part, shall not advance the opinion that the government is playing possum or deliberately trying, with details, to distract from the main issue.

I regret that lack of speaking time prevents me from analyzing in depth the arguments advanced by the government to invalidate those of Mr. Lapian,[5] who said that as a result of the differentiated pay there was an apparent tendency in the past years to lower the pensions of Indonesian soldiers. The esteemed government spokesman has not denied this but has with a broad gesture stated that it would be tiresome to the People's Council if he would analyze the quoted figures. He then submitted a table. And what conclusion can be drawn from this?—that Mr. Lapian was absolutely correct. The table of the esteemed government spokesman indicates that over the years the pensions of the Indonesian soldiers have been lowered across the board. To give a few examples: pensions of Indonesian soldiers first class were lowered from 380 to 225 guilders, of Indonesian sergeants second class from 560 to 450 guilders, sergeants first class from 900 to 750 guilders, while pensions of European soldiers have increased from 700 to 800 guilders and that of brigadiers from 784 to 900 guilders.

I repeat my regret that I am not getting the opportunity to examine in detail the statement of the esteemed government spokesman,[6] because this would mean a complete refutation of his arguments. I am thus limiting myself to handing you, Mr. Chairman, an amendment which plans to equalize the pay of all military personnel regardless of national origin. . . .

The amendment does not per se mean to seek an increase in the pay of the Indonesian soldiers. If the government agrees in principle with us that there should be equality and believes that the pay level of certain groups should not be raised but be lowered, the signers of the amendment have no objections to press for a decrease rather than an increase.

As I have said before, the basic issue in the amendment must not be sought in an increase of this budget item, but in the tenor of the amendment: to secure equal pay for all groups within the military.

NOTES

1. Dutch East Indies, Volksraad, *Handelingen, 1940/41,* pp. 1630-1632.
2. *Handelingen,* p. 1683.
3. *Handelingen,* pp. 1630-1632.
4. Session here pertains to the 1940/1941 session of the People's Council. Thamrin here refers to an earlier Council meeting where Lapian first brought up the question of equal pay for service personnel.
5. Thamrin was twice interrupted and admonished that the speaking time allocated him was running out.
6. Thamrin was interrupted and admonished that his time was up and that he would be cut short.

Mohammad Natsir

Mohammad Natsir: Paladin and Patriot
(Born 1908)

To students of modern Indonesia, Mohammad Natsir is far better known as a modern Islamic scholar and a leader of the postwar Masjumi party, than for his brief stint (1936 to 1941) as a writer for the weekly publication *Pandji Islam*.[1] In the thirties, the journalists M. Tabrani (of the Batavia-based *Pemandangan*) or Parada Harahap (of *Bintang Timur*) undoubtedly enjoyed a wider readership than did Natsir. But Natsir's articles published under the pseudonym A. Muchlis provide an excellent survey of the problems confronting the nationalist movement in the years prior to the Japanese occupation. These included the desire and demand for more and better education and the futile but persistent request for more political participation.

Mohammad Natsir was born on July 17, 1908 in the Minangkabau area of West Sumatra; his father was an administrative official, his grandfather an *ulama,* which might account for his religious interests. In Solok, Sumatra, Natsir attended grade and junior high school during the day and the religious school in the evenings.

In 1928 he left for Bandung to study at the high school (AMS) and subsequently received his teacher's training at the H.I.K. During the prewar period, Natsir was primarily concerned with religion and education. He wrote and translated several articles and books on Islam, including two studies in Dutch (one titled *The Islamic Woman and Her Right*) and founded the Pendidikan Islam, a school system in which he himself taught for a number of years.

He joined several Islamic organizations, to wit: the League of Young Moslems in the early 1930s and the Persatuan Islam in 1938. In 1932 Natsir became a student of the Islamic scholar A. Hassan, who sought to bring Indonesian Islam into the twentieth century by clearing it of the cobwebs acquired by too much exposure to indigenous Indonesian beliefs.

Natsir, although greatly interested in political problems, did not enter the political arena until after the Japanese occupation. His dislike for the Japanese is clearly evident from one of the articles reprinted here, and, during the occupation years, he seriously considered working underground but instead trained *ulama* in Bandung.

He served in a number of cabinet positions during his country's struggle against the returning Dutch colonialists. When Indonesia became independent de jure he also served as prime minister.[2] Natsir's religious beliefs permeated his political actions, he saw religion as part of society and thus regarded the two as inseparable. Although he desired the establishment of a Moslem state, he was ready to allay the fears of Christians by assuring them that Indonesian Moslems would aid all who worshipped God according to their own convictions. His attitude toward the communists was far less generous, he condemned their doctrine outright.[3]

Natsir's religious beliefs made a conflict with Sukarno inevitable, and, when in the late fifties secessionist movements erupted in several parts of the archipelago, after long hesitation Natsir joined the Sumatra-based Revolutionary Republic of Indonesia and served as vice president of the rebel government.[4] In 1961 he was granted amnesty and surrendered to Sukarno. He is presently living in Jakarta.

NOTES

1. Biographical data derived from: St. Rais Alamsjah, *op. cit.*, pp. 83–102; Peter Burns, "Revelation and Revolution," (manuscript mailed to me by Mr. Mohammad Natsir) p. 175.
2. Herbert Feith, *The Decline of Constitutional Democracy in Indonesia* (Ithaca: Cornell University Press, 1964), pp. 146–176, deals with the Natsir cabinet.
3. Howard M. Federspiel, *Persatuan Islam: Islamic Reform in Twentieth-Century Indonesia* (Ithaca: Modern Indonesia Project, Cornell University, 1970), p. 179 on Christianity; p. 175 on communism.
4. *Persatuan Islam*, p. 184

Editor's Introduction:
The Quest for Education

Education was an integral part of the nationalist movement. It had provided the impetus for a national awakening and had made a small privileged group (the recipients of that education) acutely aware of their humiliating position as members of an oppressed nation.

When, in the beginning of the twentieth century, the colonial government slowly increased the number of schools and the Indonesians admitted to these, the value of western education became apparent to many. But instruction provided by the government and the missionaries simply did not suffice to meet the demand.

Indonesian nationalists resolved to establish private schools, not only to educate but to influence young minds as well. The private schools can be divided into two groups, those based on western foundations (the religious Muhammadijah schools and the schools of the political organizations fell in this category), and those based on traditional Indonesian values (the Taman Siswo schools founded in 1923 by Ki Hadjar Dewantoro). The colonial government looked askance at these private schools, and many led a very precarious existence for they were subject to raids and constant harassment. In 1933 governmental policy toward private schools changed from repressive to preventive, but the determined opposition by Indonesians under the leadership of Ki Hadjar Dewantoro, wholly unexpected by the colonial government, forced recission of the ordinance.[1]

But harassment persisted. And therefore it is not surprising that private schools often experienced great difficulty in securing teachers.

Our Educational System Lacks Teachers![2]
(May 1938)

> Now I am advocating education, but later I may not be able to educate my children.

This is the reason advanced by an alumnus of the government's H.I.K., who was once a leader of the teachers' organization in our country. He left his teaching position and became a postal clerk. To his colleagues who asked why he changed jobs, he replied with the opening statement above.

If we study the statement there is more to it than meets the eye. Someone completed an H.I.S. education, was selected to continue at a MULO and then the H.I.K., graduated and received a diploma, worked actively in the young teachers' association, but suddenly felt compelled to leave the classroom and the students to exchange his job for work in a post office.

There are two possible explanations. Either this gentlemean never had the calling to become a teacher but was forced to attend the teachers' training school until he had his diploma, then realized that this work was incompatible with his nature, to a point where the classroom became like a prison. Thus he resigned, or this gentleman wanted for many years to become a teacher but realized that his income did not correspond with what he had previously envisaged and was inadequate to support the family in the manner that he desired. He discovered that the salary would not be sufficient to cover the cost of his children's education. Meanwhile because a better job was available, he tendered his resignation and changed positions.

In both instances we wish the gentleman "Good luck!"

This matter would not be of concern to us if it were merely a personal one. However, this example provides us with a picture of present conditions in our society.

As we know, those who operate schools, each year, have a hard time recruiting teachers. The existing teachers' training schools, both in Java and in the outer provinces, cannot meet the demand for teachers. It is estimated that each year only about 20 percent of the demand is satisfied and with considerable difficulty. Actually a senior in a teachers' training school is, in the coming months, assured of a position whether he receives his diploma or not.

Every year the situation is felt more keenly. And barring miscalculations the shortage will increase. There are several reasons:

1. The schools which do not have enough classrooms will build more, thus increasing the demand for teachers each year.

2. People will increase their efforts to establish schools when they become aware of the need for more education.

3. In times of crisis, when the government cannot absorb all graduates of the H.I.K., many of our private schools will hire them but for wages much lower than what they would receive from the government. We do not want to make sweeping generalizations—naturally there are exceptions—but we can say that in these cases many of our teachers will certainly return to work for the government when the opportunity permits. In 1938-1939 the government will gradually resume hiring H.I.K. graduates, and we can say that within two or three months most of them will be hired. We can count on our fingers the few who will be reluctant to leave their work with the people,[3] which does not provide a sufficient income and carries no pension.

All this contributes to an acute shortage of teachers in our private schools. Who will remain in these schools? Those who do not have a government certificate; those who, in their youth, never dreamed of a life in luxury as a civil servant; those who are aware of the people's needs[4] and who do not measure their skills and sacrifices in terms of government salary and the like; those who have the fortitude to bear hardships together; and those who have the strength to stay despite attractive compensations on the other side, which can offer a bigger salary.

How many of our young men at present have this attitude? Not many. How many teachers' training schools at present emphasize this attitude and these ideals? Very few indeed.

Meanwhile our people who thirst for knowledge are deprived and are incessantly waiting for the intellectuals to graduate from the H.I.K. or the government's teachers' schools. Once in a while they feel someone will join them; hoping that they will be; fearing that they may not be. They are proud when they hear Mr. so-and-so has received his assistant teaching credentials and Mr. so-and-so has now his teaching credentials, as proud as when they hear that Mr. so-and-so has become an engineer, another a lawyer, and another a medical doctor, and so forth, in the hope that they will receive assistance and guidance for their struggle which lacks everything. Often, however, they hope in vain. . . . Besides, those they believe are on their side will leave too, their job unfinished. This tragedy is not concocted but is rather common in our society. It is a calamity in the struggle of the common people, who are becoming aware but are still weak.

Let me ask, how can we revitalize the economy and the political movement among the millions of our people, when even less than 5 percent are literate? On what foundation can be built our economic and political structure when millions of our people are as yet unable to read?

The late Dr. G. J. Nieuwenhuis upon his return from the Philippines, where he studied the educational system, said: "A nation cannot make progress unless among its people are teachers who are willing to make sacrifices!"

This group of young people does exist in Filipino society, and this is one of the reasons the Philippines have progressed more rapidly than our country.

What did Gokhale, the famous Indian leader, do when he returned from the university, where he obtained his doctorate in mathematics? Rather than accepting a well-paying job with the British government he immediately became involved in education and the nationalist movement, although it provided a meager income. This great leader was not concerned that later he would not be able to educate his own children because he wanted to educate his poor people.

We hope that this overview will stimulate our young men who wish to serve their country and nation. Education! This is a field which now and in the near future faces an acute shortage of personnel. This is a field which greatly needs help. Give your efforts, young men, for the education of our people, the source of all the intellect and progress of the nation. The work is difficult and requires fortitude. If you, young men, are not willing to face hardships, difficulties, and troubles, who will. . . ?

Let us hope that our elders may prevail upon their offspring to join the nationalist movement. And encourage them to enroll in the existing teachers' training schools, whether the government's or some other, idealistically with the purpose of working for the people, not behind the windows of their offices. And that our elders may increase our private schools if there is now a shortage of places in the government's teachers' training schools. Even if these schools increase ten or fifteen times, it still will not be sufficient for the millions of our people.

NOTES

1. Pluvier, *Overzicht,* pp. 52-57.
2. From M. Natsir, *Capita Selecta I* (Bandung: W. van Hoeve, 1954), pp. 62-65. Indonesian title "Perguruan Kita Kekurangan Guru," originally published in *Pandji Islam.*
   Translated with the permission of M. Natsir. The greater part of this article was translated by Mr. Peter Ananda, Southeast Asia Bibliographer, University of California at Berkeley.
3. Natsir here refers to work with the Indonesian people as contrasted with working for the colonial government as a teacher.
4. A novel *Buiten het Gareel* by Mrs. Suwarsi Djojopuspito (Utrecht: W. de Haan, n.d.), deals with the so-called wild schools and the plight of the teachers at these schools. Although as a novel it is a failure (it has no plot), the depiction of the *Zeitgeist* is outstanding.

Editor's Introduction:
Political Concerns of the Early Forties

On January 6, 1941, Mohammad Husni Thamrin, Deputy Chairman of the People's Council, was placed under house arrest and his home searched. No official charges were filed. Thamrin, who was ill with malaria died at his home five days after the arrest. The government never issued an explanation for its unprecedented action.

There were rumors that Thamrin, a highly successful merchant, had established more than business relations with the Japanese and had been disloyal to the colonial government. The Indonesian people reacted angrily and acrimoniously to the arrest. Thousands flocked to Thamrin's funeral to demonstrate their devotion to the man who, for so many years, had pleaded their cause in the People's Council and to show their disapproval of the government's action.

In the following two articles Natsir rejects all charges of disloyalty reputed to be present within the nationalist movement and conveys some of the concerns confronting the conscious segment of the Indonesian population.

Political Standpoint of M. H. Thamrin[1]
(January 1941)

AS YET UNCLEAR

The political philosophy of Thamrin and his party is different from the position we, Moslems, have adopted. At best it is comparable to two parallel lines—not one—existing separately. We have never concealed this. However, this is not the subject of our present discussion. As for the soul of the deceased we pray to the Almighty, may the Lord forgive all his sins and accept his good deeds, amen.

The incident of the house search cannot possibly be closed with the death of the searched victim, because the victim occupied the position of Deputy Chairman of the People's Council, which its chairman called the main representative body in the Kingdom of the Netherlands today.[2] The house search was not merely a police measure but concerned the policy of the government in a much broader sense. Unless the suspicion was well founded the risk of the mentioned search was considerable. But, if no evidence was found that the searched victim committed a serious wrong, the search might have hurt the government's prestige. It is as yet unclear what prompted the government to undertake such an extreme step.

The only official announcement of the RPD, official information service,[3] was that the issue involved a copy of a letter. Even though the letter, which was a personal one, may have contained words that insulted the dignity of the government in London, it does not prove that Thamrin was plotting to overthrow the government. The Dutch press, too, was sharply critical of the government in London (see, for instance, the writings of Dr. van Blankenstein-Villanus-, several months ago).

Briefly, everything in this case is extremely murky. And unless there is an explicit official explanation, no person has the right to accuse and falsely suspect the deceased. A clear and factual explication from the government is imperative.

It is absolutely necessary to issue such a statement as soon as possible, to stop the doubts, suspicions and confusion of various groups for they constitute a danger to the present peace of mind.

We can already see the risk the government takes in waiting too long to issue an explanation. The Dutch press, in particular the *Java Bode,* is so bold as to maintain that the late Thamrin should just have been interned. *AID,* a newspaper,[4] assumed that Thamrin clearly wanted to play the role of an Indonesian Wang Ching-wei and establish contact with Japan, as Wang Ching-wei had forsaken Chiang Kai-shek and gone over to Japan to become the tool of the Japanese government. . . ! Briefly, as long as no concise explanation is issued there will be suspicion and conjecture.

It is even more dangerous when these suspicions give rise to theories expounding why Thamrin did what he is suspected of.

Algemeen Indies Dagblad for instance stated among others:

> If on the day of Thamrin's death we asked why he strayed from his patriotic course, the answer can only be: because of disappointment. Disappointment in his and his political friends' recent efforts for constitutional reforms.

We need not elaborate on a theory based upon far-fetched suspicions. But it is necessary to emphasize and caution that such hypotheses are injurious; we acknowledge that possibly these theories emerged because no official explanation has emanated from the government. Unless this is provided, people are apparently not satisfied and feel the need to draw conclusions. Originally it was assumed that Thamrin once sought or wanted to seek political contact with Japan. From that conjecture arose the question, "Why?" This quickly led to another assumption, "He was disappointed."

Once again, to dispel toying with this kind of guesswork which may considerably impair the feeling of unity needed between the government and the people, it is imperative that the government, without delay, furnishes information based on sufficient evidence. Either "Prove the accusation with adequate data," or, "Clear Thamrin's name altogether from the accusations and suspicions."

We must pool our thoughts and efforts. However, our thoughts and efforts cannot possibly be united when they are disturbed by continuous doubts such as the present ones.

DISAPPOINTMENT

We return to the problem of *teleurstelling,* disappointment. This word is not new. It was first publicly used when Wiwoho, as spokesman for the initiators of the three-motion proposal, and many other members of the People's Council were, according to their explanation, greatly disappointed with the government's reply to their request. We all know this.

But this was not confined to the Indonesians only.

D. M. G. Koch, former member of the Revision Commission of 1920 wrote in *Critiek en Opbouw* about Dr. Levelt's response,[5] paragraph 2, among others:

> The explanation advanced by Dr. Levelt on the democratization of the structure of the government of the Netherlands Indies, is considered *'irritant gepraat'*, infuriating talk![6]

Mr. Koch asked:

> Who is surprised that members of the People's Council demonstrate irritability? Must they not get the feeling that they are treated as half-educated people whose political ideals can be talked away with cunning phraseology and big words? That the mood within the indigenous circles is now worse than before May 10, may be attributed to statements like those of Mr. Levelt.

... Here and there we deliberately cut the translation a little but it still gives a clear indication that among the Dutch quite a few experienced *geprikkelde stemming* (irritable mood) over the explanation of the government's spokesman on the country's ideals . . . .

But there are different kinds of disappointment.

We do not know what was on Thamrin's mind at the end of his life. And besides we do not wish to interfere in the government's investigation now in progress. It is far from our intention to carry out a plea on behalf of the deceased; it was not proven that he had already been arrested.

However, if the white press at this crucial time exerts the right to suspect and guess, we feel the need to pose several questions which must be considered before people can form an opinion on the subject.

Anyone who has followed the debates in the People's Council in the latter part of last year must surely know that members of the Indonesian group, in particular those who initiated the three-motion proposal,[7] although they were greatly disappointed, they did not give up hope. Only a few weeks after their disappointment did they resume the discussion. Even though their debates reflected their feelings of exasperation this was better than keeping silent, penting up their emotions inside. Consequently the government's spokesman was dumbfounded but pleased when he saw that the members of the Indonesian group were once more ready to resume debate on the vital issue of the structure of the government.

And when the Indonesian group saw that there was not going to be a change in the government's position they still remained hopeful. But the feeling of anger was heard in their speeches and they again proposed a new motion; they still sought a modus vivendi, a compromise in which both sides would give and take. This was the motion signed by Sutardjo, Tadjuddin Noor, Soangkupon, Kasimo, Thamrin, and Mogot, which proposed that:

1. Membership of the People's Council should be increased to one hundred.
2. The budget should be decided by the governor-general in conjunction with the People's Council and should no longer need the approval of the Dutch parliament.
3. The power of the governor-general to issue emergency laws must be abolished.
4. The right of investigation and questioning must be granted to the People's Council without any limitations.

We bring this to the fore to illustrate that although there is a sense of exasperation, the Indonesian representatives in the council, over whom the late Thamrin exercised considerable influence, were willing to seek a compromise wherever possible. This is the situation in the People's Council. But not merely there.

In GAPI,[8] the federation of the Indonesian political movement, in which Thamrin and his party played a leading role, voices expressing disappointment were quite audible. Yet, basically we are convinced that GAPI will proceed along legal routes. They are still waiting for a meeting with the Visman Commission. And if a meeting between GAPI and the Visman Commission has not yet taken place this is not the fault of the GAPI.[9] In the meantime GAPI continues to complete its program of action. The latest announcement from the secretariat explains succinctly that efforts to promote the ideals implementing *Indonesia Berparlamen* will proceed by legal means, within the framework of the country's laws.[10]

This illustrates the attitude and spirit of the Indonesian group, within and without the People's Council, not only before but even after the people's representatives received such a disappointing response from the government. Disappointment breeds disappointment, but the work must continue in the same direction.

This direction is: Faith that the government will gradually open its eyes and its heart for their just and important demands, which is important for the common welfare, in particular, during this unfortunate time of war. Disappointed or not, angry or not, even though the political struggle is fraught with anger and disappointment, these do not dominate the attitude and spirit of the Indonesian political circle now.

The most influential and apparent aspect of their struggle is the strong and continued search for a legal and workable means of just and sincere cooperation with the nation's government to obtain an improvement of their position within the framework of the state's structure. This improvement in status may well be the only way to elevate the spirit and to instill inspiration necessary to repulse all dangers which may strike from within or without.

This is the current situation, the *grondtoon,* the tendency of their current action and of their political struggle, whether at the bottom of the movement or in the top echelons among such leaders as Thamrin, Sutardjo, Wiwoho, and others. And before drawing conclusions based on the harmful disappointment theory, there is an important factor the government should take into consideration: the evidence of considerable goodwill to cooperate.

NOTES

1. From: M. Natsir, *Capita Selecta,* pp. 333–342. Originally published in *Pandji Islam,* in Indonesian, as "Pendirian Politik M. H. Thamrin."
   Translated with permission of M. Natsir. The greater part of this article was translated by Mr. Peter Ananda, Southeast Asia Bibliographer of the University of California at Berkeley.
2. After the fall of the Netherlands in May 1940 the People's Council was considered the main, remaining representative body in the Kingdom of the Netherlands.
3. *R*(ijks) *P*(ubliciteits) *D*(ienst), Government Publicity Service, the official information service in the Indies.
4. *Java Bode* and *A*(lgemeen) *I*(ndisch) *D*(agblad), were Dutch newspapers published in Batavia and Bandung respectively.
5. *Critiek en Opbouw,* a weekly magazine on political problems published between 1938–1941 in Bandung, was highly critical of colonial policy.
6. Dr. H. J. Levelt was the government's spokesman who reported on the three-motion proposal. His reply was (August 25, 1940) that the time was not propitious to introduce fundamental changes. They would have to wait until the Netherlands parliament could discuss them.
7. Three-motion proposal: were the Motion Thamrin for the official use of the words Indonesian and Indonesia; the Motion Sutardjo for an Indies citizenship; and the Motion Wiwoho for more autonomy.
8. GAPI, Gabungan Politik Indonesia, was a federation of Indonesian political groups, established on the initiative of M. H. Thamrin.
9. The Visman Commission was instituted to study political reforms after the three-motion proposal was rejected. GAPI at first refused to meet with members of the commission. Pluvier, *Overzicht,* pp. 180–181.
10. Movement for an Indonesian parliament.

Is There "Wang Ching-Wei-ism" in Indonesia? "No!" We Respond.[1]
(February 1941)

"Let's hope that the banana does not bear fruit twice."

We have already discussed this sort of theory advanced by some of the white press which states that the late Thamrin traded national politics with politics à la Wang Ching-wei; it was—they say—because he was profoundly disappointed and had given up hope of reaching an accord between the Indonesian and the government's points of view. . . . Nevertheless among the Indonesian leaders, both within and outside the People's Council, a feeling of hopelessness, as depicted by the white press, could not possibly have existed; but it cannot be denied that there was concern about the distressing result of the exchange of thought in the People's Council.

Every Indonesian somewhat informed on politics regardless of whether he is a great leader, such as a People's Council member, will no doubt vehemently reject any theory resembling Wang Ching-wei-ism, for this is very harmful to Indonesia. And if a leader would inject the tenor of Wang Ching-wei into the Indonesian nationalist movement, he would certainly be rebuked, for it is at variance with the spirit and essence of the Indonesian nationalist movement.

If we want to describe the current mood of the Indonesian nationalist movement, we must first put the matter in its proper perspective.

However, the absence of a Wang Ching-wei spirit within the Indonesian movement does not mean that any problem can be easily solved.

We live in a country that is at war. To attend to all that is important for that war, we must mobilize all of our existing forces as efficiently as possible. In unifying the strength and power of the Indonesian people of all walks of life, hating the enemy is not enough; it is not enough that the people want no more dealings with a third power or reject outside intervention.

What is needed is the desire to live until death do us part, *le désir de vivre ensemble,* the willingness to bear hardship together as a group, to strive for the same goal, bound by fate, a group with common interests. And to generate this desire we need proof of goodwill from the government. This goodwill implies giving a greater share of the government of the country to the people. The people and the government of Indonesia at present are faced with solving this problem. On this issue Indonesians of all walks of life have the same opinion.

About half of the white press argues this way:

> The Government now works energetically for the betterment of the people, namely, for the improvement of the people's welfare. The Government has introduced a proposal to abolish *herendienst*[2]; the Government has already increased the number of schools for the people and is willing to give aid to the unaccredited schools.

We acknowledge all this and we appreciate it. But one should not exaggerate in evaluating and determining the impact that abolition of the *herendienst* has on people's attitudes. It is not our intention to belittle the appreciation of the government's measure, which is insignificant compared to what the people have for years demanded. But we must make clear that in the present political situation these steps do not carry great weight.

It is like making adequate advance preparations for a highly esteemed visitor. We go to meet this noble guest at the station, but he does not arrive. We are forced to wait for several hours even half a day. It is only natural that our desire changes to anger and frustration. And if suddenly the guest should appear a day late he will not find happy and beaming faces. At best he will be welcomed with a cold handshake and a strained smile. This is to illustrate the people's reaction to measures such as abolition of the *herendienst.* We may decry people's reaction, but psychologically it is inevitable. Governing a country and mass psychology are two inseparable things.

Concluding our discussion we must emphasize that:

1. The spirit of the Indonesian nationalist movement is, Praise the Lord, pure and free from the vermin of Wang Ching-wei and the like.

2. Nevertheless it must be recognized that the Indonesian people lack the enthusiasm for making sacrifices and for mobilizing their efforts, imperative to confront the present and future dangers of war.

3. The government's stand in declining to give and take on the three-

motion proposal on the governmental structure introduced in the past session of the People's Council does not promote the spirit of *lotsverbondenheid*[3] among the groups of residents here. On the contrary!

4. The government's suggestion that even minor and insignificant changes in the political structure should only be discussed after the war is considered by the Indonesian groups (and equally in Dutch circles) like putting the horse behind the buggy. . . .

5. The *kesatrian* theory à la Dr. Tjipto may be good and sound patriotism,[4] however, it found little response in the profoundest feelings of the Indonesian people in general and was not welcomed within the Indonesian nationalist movement. On the contrary such a patriotic gesture is, in view of present-day conditions, discouraging and greatly obstructs the realization of the spirit of *lotsverbondenheid,* which is imperative in evoking the strength and energy of the tens of millions of people.

All this must be achieved by putting things in their proper perspective.

Recently the People's Council started a discussion on the second motion regarding the governmental structure, which was introduced by Mr. Sutardjo and was cosigned by Messrs. Tadjuddin Noor, Soangkupon, Kasimo, Thamrin, and Mogot, who have become a unified group that can be considered to represent the various interest groups among the Indonesian people. Perhaps by next week we can comment on the debates in the People's Council on this issue. Can our wounds be healed?

Or could it be that the banana bears fruit twice?

NOTES

1. From: M. Natsir, *Capita Selecta,* pp. 339-342. Indonesian title originally published in *Pandji Islam* as "Adakah 'Wang Ching Weism' di Indonesia? 'Tidak!' Sahut Kita." Translated with permission of M. Natsir. The greater part of this article was translated by Mr. Peter Ananda, Southeast Asia Bibliographer at the University of California at Berkeley.
2. *Herendienst,* unpaid labor by native men performed for the government.
3. *Lotsverbondenheid* (bound together by fate), here a feeling of sharing a similar destiny.
4. Kesatrya theory à la Dr. Tjipto. Dr. Tjipto Mangunkusumo, a fiery nationalist, was interned by the Dutch in 1929 and released in 1940. He advocated to suspend fighting an enemy in need (the Netherlands were occupied by Germany in 1940), like a true Ksatrya, the warrior caste who were in Javanese mythology noble knights.

PART III
THE REVOLUTIONARIES

Dr. Mohammad Hatta

Mohammad Hatta: Scholar and Statesman (Born 1902)

Mohammad Hatta rose to prominence in the Nationalist Movement during his eleven years' stay in the Netherlands.[1] As a board member of the student organization Perhimpunan Indonesia, he contributed to their publication, *Indonesia Merdeka,* many articles pertaining to problems confronting the nationalist cause. Most of his writings reflect his calm reasoning, his clarity and acuity of mind; Hatta had no use nor need for complex and confusing verbiage, illogic was beyond his ken.

The son of a Minangkabau *ulama,* Hatta was born on August 12, 1902 near Bukittinggi, Sumatra's West Coast, where he received his grade school, junior high, and religious education. He became interested in the political issues of his day as a teenager and joined the League of Young Sumatrans. Because there was no high school in Sumatra, Hatta left for Batavia to complete his studies and proceeded to the Netherlands to study at the commercial school in Rotterdam which offered courses beyond the junior college level. Hatta planned to stay but four years, however, when the school commenced offering courses in political economy (in addition to business administration) he decided to remain until he obtained his degree (doctorandus, completing all requirements except the dissertation).

In 1927, while still a student, Hatta had joined the League against Imperialism and Colonial Oppression, and at one of its conventions met and befriended the Indian nationalist J. Nehru. Hatta's activities in the league led, at the instigation of the colonial government, to his arrest on charges of incitement to revolt against the legal government. At his trial Hatta presented a brilliant plea in his own defense entitled *Indonesia Free;* he was acquitted for lack of evidence.[2]

In 1932 Hatta returned to Indonesia and joined Pendidikan Indonesia, a political organization seeking to foster political awareness among the people through training sessions in small groups. Among its other goals were the abolition of a class society and of private property. The government looked askance at this organization, and Hatta's arrest (simultaneous with that of S. Sjahrir's, the chairman of the organization) came as no surprise. He spent one year in jail before he was exiled to Boven Digul, and subsequently spent six years in Banda. Shortly before the Japanese invasion the colonial government brought Hatta back to Java.

Hatta had as little sympathy for the Japanese rulers as he had had for the Dutch: at an open rally on December 8, 1942 he spoke the words: "Indonesian youth would rather see Indonesia sink to the bottom of the sea than have it ruled again by an alien power." Obviously such a statement did not endear him to the Japanese.

In August 1945 the sudden Japanese surrender gave Sukarno and Hatta the opportunity to proclaim Indonesia's independence. As president and vice-president, the duumvirate Sukarno-Hatta successfully directed the struggle against the returning colonial power. And Hatta, with whom the Dutch had refused to negotiate in 1945, chaired the Indonesian delegation to the Round Table Conference in The Hague which at last gave Indonesians sovereignty over their own country.

In August 1950 with the proclamation of the Indonesian Republic, Hatta became Indonesia's first vice-president. He resigned in 1956, stating that he had planned to serve for only two years. The address he delivered shortly after his resignation at Gadja Mada University in Jogjakarta to receive an honorary doctorate indicated that basic differences of opinion with the course independent Indonesia had taken were the real reasons.[3] In Hatta's opinion a national parliament could not possibly make unanimous decisions (as was advocated by Sukarno), for this would result in chaos. Hatta believed that training for democracy should start at the local, regency level.

Hatta's departure from the vice-presidency permanently removed a truly great Indonesian from the Indonesian political scene. Since his self-imposed political retirement, he has devoted himself entirely to writing and lecturing.

NOTES

1. Biographical data derived from St. Rais Alamsjah, *10 Orang Indonesia Terbesar Sekarang* (Bukittingi, Djakarta, Padang: Mutiara, 1952), pp. 31–48; M. Hatta, *Verspreide Geschriften* (Djakarta, Amsterdam, Surabaya: C. P. J. van der Peet, 1952), pp. 7–17.

2. J. TH. Petrus Blumberger, *De Nationalistische Beweging in Nederlandsch Indie* (Haarlem: Tjeenk Willink, 1931) pp. 192-196.
3. M. Hatta, *Past and Present* (Ithaca, N.Y.: Modern Indonesia Project, Cornell University, 1960), pp. 14-16.

Editor's Introduction:
An Advocate of Noncooperation

Cooperation or noncooperation was the issue discussed among the nationalist leaders in the twenties and thirties. In the early twenties the harsh policies of Governor-General Fock (1921-1926) had turned many moderates, such as Hadji Agus Salim, away from the government.

Fock's successor was Jonkheer de Graeff, a diplomat who had been Dutch ambassador to the United States. He held out the prospect of a more accommodating colonial policy expressing the wish to work with the nationalists and professing a sympathy for their goals.

During all of the colonial era Hatta remained adamantly for noncooperation. Here he gives some of his reasons for rejecting cooperation.

Manifest Cooperation[1]

According to Aneta,[2] a political demonstration took place in Batavia a few days ago. All the Indonesian members of the municipal council have resigned because alderman Thamrin was not designated deputy mayor, although under the seniority rule and in keeping with precedent he should have been considered. Mayor Meyroos adopted the view that "at present in an Indies municipality established along western lines the position of mayor could only be occupied by a Westerner," whereupon he recommended Mr. Leeuwis.

The *Java Bode*[3] considered it understandable that Mr. Thamrin felt hurt by this slight and pointed out that for some time Bandung had an Indonesian deputy mayor, Mr. Darna Kusuma, against whom the Dutch community never objected.

This collective resignation of the Indonesian members of the Batavia municipality is regarded by some as "noncooperation."

What is the truth of this?

Participation in the proceedings of the People's Council, municipal, and other local councils rests in a majority of cases on the principle of cooperation. Indonesian politicians who take their seats in these councils are not motivated by the principle of obstruction but by the belief that the alien ruler is willing to lead Indonesia gradually toward independence or at least autonomy. With a policy of cooperation they believe they can realize their surrogate idea, namely, the gradual replacement of Dutchmen by Indonesians in all ranks of the colonial administration. They fail to assess reality in that the alien Dutch ruler will never voluntarily free the rich colony from the Netherlands which, on the basis of this political retention alone, is not inclined to let anyone replace him. This would signify the liquidation of the Dutch ruler's power position.

The Indonesian alderman Thamrin is now passed over for the position of deputy mayor. This was not based on personal incompetence, but because he is Indonesian. One does not want an Indonesian heading a municipality, not even temporarily, in the event of the mayor's absence. One feels that this insult to race feelings should be answered by collective resignation. And in this lies the tragedy of the cooperation policy.

For what is now the most significant characteristic of this demonstration, something the persons involved may not have been aware of?

Overtly it is an expression of hurt feelings but in essence it is a protest against the nonrecognition of loyalty by the white masters. A protest against the fact that one is, in the eyes the alien ruler, not yet loyal enough to merit their confidence. A conspicuous attempt to make the white possessors of power recognize their own good faith.

Therefore we should not see this collective resignation of the Indonesian members of the municipal council of Batavia as an act of noncooperation but as manifest cooperation.

It is reminiscent at times of a policy of *mau minta di budjuk*.[4]

Noncooperation can only be effective when one is convinced that a policy of cooperation is basically misleading, for knowledge as well as experience prove that the alien ruler will never voluntarily renounce his millions in annual profit.

To the fundamental noncooperators participation in the proceedings of the People's Council and other councils signifies harm to their own national cause. Taking part in these councils, which have nothing in common with popular representation, sanctions governmental organizations that plan to "keep kids happy" evidenced by their composition and powers.

By not attaching any value to these fabrications of the alien ruler, one gives the Indonesian people self-confidence, stimulates its urge to act, and demonstrates to the masses that the white man is not indispensable in Indonesia. What a source of power do we tap here!

In his review in *The People* of November 14, 1929,[5] Mr. J. E. Stokvis justifies this resignation of the Indonesian members of the municipality and describes this as incidental noncooperation. Noncooperation as a tactical weapon, such as we espouse, he rejects. But occasionally used and as an extreme means of resistance, it is, according to him, in a colonial situation sometimes unavoidable and also useful.

On this naive positing of the problem, we would only like to ask: How long should incidental noncooperation last? Just imagine that the Dutch faction of councilmen will not yield on the appointment of Mr. Thamrin as deputy mayor—which is a more likely presumption—does one then voluntarily return to the council?[6]

And if so, what is the meaning of this demonstration of collective resignation? What does all this policy of *memonggok* mean? Above all does this really indicate integrity?

If not what is left of "occasional?" Does this not signify in the long run a conversion to the real noncooperation, albeit prompted by reasons different from those of the fundamental noncooperators?

In this case one could only return to the municipal council when the opponents are ready to mend the blow dealt to the race sentiment. On the whole one can easily calculate that the policy of cooperation, with an occasional noncooperational slant, is only useful in securing small concessions in politically insignificant matters. But as a weapon to gain basic concessions, it is completely unsound and resembles more self-mockery than self-respect.

In the present colonial relationships where the Indonesian people, the masses, have no voice at all in the regulation of their lives and in the destiny of their fate, noncooperation is the only correct weapon.

NOTES

1. From: M. Hatta, *Past and Present*, pp. 439–441. Originally published in Dutch as "Demonstrative Cooperatie," in *Indonesia Merdeka*, 1929. Translated with the permission of M. Hatta.
2. Dutch newsagency in Batavia.
3. Dutch newspaper published in Batavia.
4. *Mau minta di budjuk* means "we are asking for recognition."
5. J. E. Stokvis, Dutch journalist and Social Democrat, member of the People's Council 1923–1929 and 1930–1931; member of the Tweede Kamer (lower house of the Dutch parliament) 1937–1946.
6. Alderman Thamrin became second deputy mayor of the Batavia municipality and first deputy mayor in 1930 when the incumbent resigned.

Editor's Introduction:
A Nationalist Comments on an "Ethical" Governor-General

Governor-General de Graeff, who took office in September, 1926, shortly after his inauguration was faced with the eruption of revolts (instigated by communists) in Banten and Sumatra's West Coast. The uprisings were brutally suppressed; many of the instigators were executed, and thousands were exiled to the morass place, Boven Digul in New Guinea.

However, the governor-general subsequently appointed a commission to study the cause of the revolts. The reports of the investigation were highly critical of administration policies, placing the blame squarely on the government.

Hatta's view of de Graeff is highly perceptive. The governor-general was a vacillating figure who, trying to please nationalists and Dutch alike, only succeeded in alienating both groups. A lawyer by training, de Graeff was forced by circumstances to resort to political, extralegal, and arbitrary measures—such as banishment of politically dangerous persons—embittering many Indonesians. By conservative Dutchmen he was mockingly called an "ethical" governor-general.

Governor-General De Graeff and the Indonesian Independence Movement[1]

When in the fall of 1926 at a public session of the People's Council, Jonkheer de Graeff took over the function and dignity of the position of governor-general from Mr. Dirk Fock, he said that one of the most important aspects of the new administration's policy would be "to win back the confidence lost" by the Indonesian people in the government. Thereby he did not fail to criticize indirectly the fist-policy of his predecessor by saying that fighting communism should not degenerate into systematic persecution. And de Graeff continued that he would not be a genuine Dutchman if he did not have respect for Indonesian nationalist ideals.

This last statement must be somewhat appealing to those who do not carry their Indonesian nationalist heart in the right place. They forget that caution should be observed in dealing with a diplomat who tries to accomplish his goal by subtle means not basically repugnant to an opponent. On fundamental colonial policy, namely, the preservation of Dutch power in Indonesia, there definitively exists no difference of opinion between Fock and de Graeff. They differ only in tactics that are employed. Whereas Mr. Fock thought to maintain Dutch power, faced by a growing independence movement, by an iron-fist policy, a policy of sheer force, Jonkheer de Graeff was of the opinion that this aim could be accomplished by an ethical-coax-policy, which would abate the revolutionary sentiment of the Indonesians and rock the nationalist movement to sleep. Did not the gentleman-diplomat, the Count of Limburg Stirum, during his administration successfully pursue this policy? But Jonkheer de Graeff forgot that present conditions in Indonesia are different from those of ten years ago.

The [weekly] *Indonesia Merdeka* (no. 4, 1926, p. 98), a publication of the Perhimpunan Indonesia, remarked appropriately in reference to the appointment of Jonkheer de Graeff as governor-general:

> The white press in Holland and Indonesia has devoted a long series of articles to the reinstatement of the ethical-coax-policy whereby predictions are made on Jonkheer de Graeff's chances. But this nervous maneuvering will accomplish nothing to prevent our effective growth, which is constantly gaining momentum. The alien ruler, who in his simplicity believes that we are so childish that we could once more be buttered up ethically by a crafty diplomat and could be sidetracked but one inch from the direction we have taken, will be sorely disappointed. Time will teach them!

The course of events of the past two years has demonstrated the accuracy of this prediction. This is inevitable, because when a different person becomes the officeholder the system itself remains unchanged. Whoever occupies this position, whatever his personal, political, and social convictions may be, he is the responsible chief official in charge, whose duty it is to maintain unimpaired Dutch power in Indonesia.

The treacherousness of the sweet-sounding words of Jonkheer de Graeff soon became evident when he rebuffed the often-voiced wishes from Indonesian nationalist circles to abrogate the notorious Articles 153 (*bis* and *ter*) and 161 (*bis*) of the Indies Penal Code, because these nipped in the bud the freedom of action of the Indonesian political organizations and trade unions. If Jonkheer de Graeff had been serious in his effort to regain the confidence of the Indonesian people it would have been the obvious move to abolish these hated articles born in the terror period of Mr. Fock. Thus one can surmise what the real essence is of the announced policy of "regaining confidence." Later it will become evident that the policy contains little more than a, in flattering terms, pronounced hint to the Indonesian nationalists to submit to the wishes of the government and "to cooperate"; and furthermore not to pursue their nationalist aspirations beyond the limits set by the authorities.

When in November, 1926 and in January, 1927 the population of Banten and Sumatra's West Coast revolted against the government as a result of misrule and of economic and social misery, as the government commission later acknowledged, it became then clear that the "ethical" hand of Jonkheer de Graeff could hit harder than the fist of such a born tyrant as Fock.

Never has arbitrary rule been so rampant as now under his [de Graeff's] administration.

Without any form of process hundreds of people were exiled to the deep jungles of New Guinea. His "ethics" conveys that he has purposely selected one of the unhealthiest spots in the archipelago, where malaria and cholera are prevalent, as a concentration camp for his political adversaries, who, notwithstanding the Indies penal provisions that were worded as pliably as possible, could not be prosecuted under the law. That these mass banishments to Boven Digul violate the intent of the lawmaker does not concern him. Never before were the so-called exorbitant rights [powers]—the power to banish people without any form of process—applied as often as is presently the case. Actually we can no longer speak of exorbitant, that is, extraordinary, powers. For this exertion of arbitrary power, which in the language of the alien ruler is also called law, has become custom.

The best part of it occurred when the governor-general himself declared, at the opening of the People's Council in 1927, that it was not impossible that totally innocent people were among those banished. The star correspondent of the *Nieuwe Rotterdamsche Courant* spoke in the same vein in his disclosure of the unbearable and inhumane conditions in Boven Digul. Several months ago the Minister of Colonies announced in the Dutch parliament that a "careful" investigation would be carried out to determine how many innocent people were banished to this place. But the government is in no hurry to start this [investigation]. Moreover such statements give the impression that there is indeed, among those banished, a question of "guilt."

The guilty have long since been incarcerated or hanged. Precisely because those hundreds of people under the rule of law are innocent, they are exiled to Boven Digul on the specious ground that they are "dangerous to the public law and order." To what extent this was the case, the colonial government in its nervousness had no time to investigate.

After his visit to Boven Digul Dr. van Blankenstein among others, wrote:

> The administration at Tanah Merah separates the intellectuals among the interns into two large groups: a large right-wing group and a small group of irreconcilable left-wingers. The latter have been put in a new camp completely separated from the main camp by the military and administrative offices. At present there are about fourteen fundamental communists, who have had to establish their very primitive home under very dire circumstances among the slough and puddles. No one will deny that it seems like a hell, which I shall describe in more detail. Even the care of provisions was completely insufficient because the place is so hard to reach over land. . . .When I arrived in the outlying camp of the fourteen sequestered men, I thought I was in one of the terrible penal camps of the French deportation colony in Cayenne. There I saw a similar neglect of the exiled. Through a cove we reached the camp by motorboat. We found a small *pon-*

dok with a tin roof but without walls, serving fourteen people for sleeping. Then there was a clearing where the framework for a larger barrack was being erected. This was all of Boven Digul that was not flooded during high tide. Puddles were everywhere. Hygienically, in particular, as a place to live, it was appalling. The interns related that they were surveying the woods for a higher place to set up their homes. For living in that place was impossible. Indeed, there was no question about it. Two of the sequestered men were seriously ill with malaria in a condemned jail, which had been equipped as a hospital for them.

And the government spokesman for general affairs, Mr. Kiewiet de Jonge still had the temerity to declare in the People's Council that these gloomy remarks of Dr. van Blankenstein should be considered in conjunction with the fact that he was unfamiliar with conditions in the jungle (woods).

What a fine exoneration and this of one's own actions. But what kind of a mentality is hereby demonstrated? One should first have to get used to the jungle to be able to judge whether a cleared wilderness amidst puddles and morass is fit for habitation before one can observe the above-cited . . . conditions. And with a hint of indignation the administration spokesman countered Mr. Stokvis, who dared to make provoking remarks about Boven Digul in this "exalted body"—one is in this distinguished company easily offended—with the following:

> The government does not want injustice, not even with banishments. Surely Mr. Stokvis himself could have understood this.

Indeed in a colony where the law and the power of the government are one and the same thing, there can be no question of "injustice." The government can always designate the most atrocious injustice "law." Then the matter is formally settled. In a free country governed by parliamentary rules the government can be held accountable and be ousted if its actions violate the general sense of justice in the nation, but in a colonized country such as Indonesia the people have no voice to regulate the life of the society. They have no legal power to prevent illegal acts of the government. The alien ruler decides arbitrarily what constitutes justice and injustice. The only right the population has is the moral right of resistance, if the oppression becomes untenable and the grievances evermore intolerable.

It is obvious how much the heralded "policy to regain lost confidence" of Jonkheer de Graeff is at variance with the method pursued by him of "eradicating communism." One could counter that the latest revolts terrified the government, but this does not justify mass internment of people, without any form of process, to the morass places of

Boven Digul, which is an indication of revenge, an action which in itself and in the way it was executed, violated Article 37 and 38 of the Act on the Governance of the Netherlands Indies. Article 37. . . . states:

> The Governor-General can, in agreement with the Council of the Indies in the interest of public safety, assign or deny a certain place of residence in certain parts of the archipelago to persons born within the Netherlands Indies.

And naturally every normal-thinking human being could determine that with a "certain place," the lawmaker could not possibly have meant a clearing in the jungle in the midst of puddles and morass, but rather an inhabited place with culture and an economic life, because confinement is not punishment but an administrative measure. The internment provision itself presupposes that the interned can make (as previously) a reasonably adequate living in his new abode.

Now the illegality of the mass internments becomes obvious when one realizes that the conditions of the Indonesian exiles in Boven Digul are more deplorable than those of the most infamous criminals who are serving time in the various jails in Indonesia. Article 38 of the Law on the Governance of the Netherlands Indies states:

> In cases refered to in articles 35, 36 and 37 the Governor-General will only decide after the person in question has had a hearing or an opportunity for this. The hearing will be duly recorded.

The experience of the latest internments has shown that this provision, meant as a guarantee for the person in question, is merely a dead letter. Instead of hearing a defense of the accused, which requires a summons, they were simply given to sign a series of stenciled questions with answers already provided. If they refused to sign they were beaten, flogged, and denied food until they, weary with torture, finally complied. Thus Jonkheer de Graeff received his more than fifteen hundred candidates for Boven Digul. Naturally he could assert that practices such as enforced confession and political coercion took place without his knowledge and were the work of police officers, but it cannot be denied that this is taking place, or has, during his administration, and he is and remains the main culprit in these actions.

Had Governor-General de Graeff been serious with his announced policy of regaining the lost confidence of the Indonesian people, he should have consciously acted differently, rather than banish a great number of people, without any form of legal process or hearing, to the morass places in Boven Digul. For he should have had the courage to face honestly the basic causes of the revolts and try to eliminate them.

But the political vision of a viscount, who is more familiar with the daily routine of colonial bureaucracy and the higher levels of diplomacy, differs fundamentally from that of a man of the people, familiar with the needs and wishes of the population. To this aristocrat, the common people appear to be will-less objects, without feelings or thoughts of their own, whose desires he believes he can equate with that of a group of "intellectuals," who are themselves separated from the masses with whom they have no spiritual or party bonds.

It is a matter of common knowlege that the iron-fist policy of Governor-General Fock turned many of this small group of intellectuals away from the government. For opportunistic reasons they declared not to value cooperation with the government. But they never were noncooperators, in principle. When Jonkheer de Graeff mentioned regaining lost confidence, he certainly meant the confidence of these people, who were outside the the fold of the popular organizations. For he would have been very naive if he had cherished any hopes that his ethical-coax-policy could persuade the nationalist organizations to relinquish the noncooperation principle, as long as the basic tenets of the existing colonial form of government were not radically altered.

If he could win over this small group of intellectuals to government policy, then the colonial government could pride itself that in maintaining Netherlands authority it could rely on, besides the existing "backbone" of Netherlands colonial imperialism, namely, the native administration, the loyal cooperation of the intellectuals.

As a reward for their loyal attitude and their willingness to cooperate, the government held out the prospect that the seat assignment among the several racial groups in the People's Council would be changed to favor the indigenous element. Legislation was introduced stipulating that the People's Council would have thirty Indonesians, at least twenty-five Netherlanders, and three to five other Asians. This nullified the Feber Amendment of 1925, which caused so much displeasure in the ranks of the Indonesian cooperating politicians. As far as we know this proposition was accepted first by the People's Council and recently by the Second Chamber as well.[2]

It is typical of the mentality of the colonial imperialists and capitalists that they made such a commotion over this essentially insignificant change in the composition of the People's Council.

In particular in European colonial circles there existed a strong opposition against this law. No less a person than the president of the Java Bank, Mr. Trip, took the initiative to evoke a strong reaction of the white element against the government's plan. In no time he had gathered 12,995 signatures of leading tropical Dutchmen for a petition to the governor-general to postpone the partial change in the People's Council. Vital Dutch interests are said to be involved. Simultaneously the Dutch started a campaign against the governor-general. In the interests of his bread-providers, the paid president of the Indies Council of Entrepreneurs sounded alarm in his pamphlet entitled: *Het Gist in Indie* [Ferment in the Indies]. Another prominent Netherlander, Mr. P. Staal, former consul general in Calcutta, mentions in his brochure *Onze Oosterse vraagstukken getoetst aan de ervaring in Brits-Indie* [Our Oriental problems compared with the experience in British India], that the best guarantee for Dutch interests is:

> a government which resolutely demonstrates to believe in its own power which accommodates the native in minor conflicts as a just and gentle friend, but which as soon as vital interest of our own people [that is the Netherlands nation] is threatened, will not hesitate to be exclusively and inexorably, master.

A better argument for the modern colonial-robber theory could not have been found. Here Staal said something that came, as it were, from the heart of the Netherlands' capitalists and imperialists.

The reactionary white front movement at last has not missed its mark. At the opening of the People's Council in May 1928 Jonkheer de Graeff finally had to reveal his true colors by saying, "that Dutch leadership in this country will be indispensable for some time." Simultaneously he divided the nationalist movement into "evolutionary" nationalists, those who can count on the sympathy of the government, and the "revolutionary" nationalists, those who the guardian would like to seize by the throat and who will be closely watched by the government. Between the two groups a fundamental difference is said to exist. Therefore the so-called healthy nationalists were warned against the so-called destructive nationalists. The aim is obvious: to effectuate a split in the nationalist movement's goal for unity among all factions. And this unity has consolidated itself in the establishment of the Indonesian National Concentration, the PPPKI, against which the reactionary European press propagated the forming of a white front. The explanatory statement of the preliminary report to the People's Council was phrased thus: "the popular movement can only expect the sympathy of the government if they accept the premise of the continuation of Dutch leadership."

This government statement came as a shock to the ranks of the credulous moderate nationalists, who had cherished high hopes of the coaxing words of Jonkheer de Graeff when he assumed office. In reply to this government statement the intellectual association Budi Utomo, known for its loyalty, published a manifesto in which all Indonesian nationalists were admonished "to maintain unity in the struggle for national freedom." The division of "evolutionary" and "revolutionary" nationalists was deemed artificial and rejected, because it appeared a reaction of the government "to the laboriously reached unity by the majority of the nationalists organizations in the PPPKI." The manifesto concluded with the words:

> Against this threatening course only one reply is possible for every right-minded nationalist namely closer unity, tighter organization. Let us do away with differences among each other and make the PPPKI arbiter in possible conflicts. Unity of action with the slogan: toward Indonesia's freedom through indissoluble unity.

This manifesto was sensational because it emanated from the moderate association Budi Utomo and not from a revolutionary party such as the PNI or PSI. For the Indonesian noncooperators ... the statement of the governor-general is not unforeseen, because they had always expected this sooner or later. Through thorough analysis of the colonial problems, they have always understood that the highest representative of Dutch colonial power, whatever his personal opinion might be, could not have acted differently. It is the logical consequence of the colonial system, which departs from the premise that Indonesia should remain an appendage of the company of the Netherlands, in the interest of the yearly stream of millions that pour out of Indonesia to Holland.

Those who possess a sound opinion on colonial power relations cannot expect much benefit from the offer to cooperate with the government, no matter how enticing this may seem. For this cooperation, as proposed by the governor-general, boils down to an exertion of ethical force against the weak Indonesian side. It is not cooperation when the opposition party merely has to submit to government policy and its guidelines. Real cooperation can but exist on the basis of mutual compromise, for example, if the government was willing to create a new democratic election system instead of the present defective one, so that the population could have an important influence on the composition of the People's Council; if the government could further meet some of the urgent requests of the Indonesian nationalists' movement, in all its manifestations, to abolish the penal sanction, the Articles 161 *(bis)*, 153 *(bis* and *ter)* of the Indies Penal Code, which hang over the head of the nationalist and the labor union movements like Damocles' sword. But the "ethical" government will have none of this. Law and order of the Dutch colonial capitalists thereby would be disturbed. Even the proposal by Kusumo Utoyo, member of the People's Council, to appoint Indonesians, too, as mayors, was rebuffed by the government out of fear for the protests by the Dutch citizenry, who do not like to see an Indonesian at the helm of a municipality of which the Dutch form a part.

When the nationalist organizations, the PNI, and the PSI declined this specious offer, the "thoughtful," "ethical," and "poised" government appeared visibly irritated and offended. In its *Information on Subjects of General Interest,* the now-prominent PNI was mentioned:

> Under the leadership of the Bandung intellectuals the PNI has captured a prominent place in the political field. In addition to organizing the forces within their own framework they try to carry, in their wake, several other organizations. The enthusiasm of these young academicians not merely captivates the older people but inspires even more the youth with the deceptive ideal of an autonomous and independent Indonesia in the near and already visible future. The propaganda takes place systematically according to a previously composed plan drawn up by the Indonesian organization in The Hague. While such a conjunction of circumstances has undoubtedly already a suspicious side, this ultranationalist organization, in addition, has taken the standpoint that in principle it does not want to take part in the existing political life; what does exist in the political realm they ignore and in those places where their ideas and ideals find a response, the tendency develops to turn away from the regime. They are led by and attract those young forces in the native society whose national task should be to work within the framework of the government, or, at least to cooperate toward the construction of a new society.

This phraseology already typifies the attitude of the governor-general toward the Indonesian freedom movement. But in this pronouncement one also can clearly uncover his hypocrisy. There is mention of young Indonesian forces turning their back to the regime. How does Jonkheer de Graeff explain the fact that Indonesians, in spite of years of service, are rudely eliminated from the colonial administration because they openly adhere to ideals which do not please the government? Actually the government has seen to it that in the daily routine of colonial officialdom there is no place for a revolutionary Indonesian nationalist. The colonial government treats its Indonesian officials as objects of the authorities or as wage-slaves, which is totally different [from the policy pursued] in the free Netherlands.

In the framework of the colonial system it is logical that the PNI, in particular, is out of grace with Governor-General de Graaff, because it is the party which consistently advocates freedom for Indonesia. In the People's Council the government's spokesman for general affairs expressed himself thus, pointing, in particular, to the activities of the PNI, that the government would not hesitate to take action against those whose words could result in jeopardizing Dutch authority. Naturally the government itself determines when this would be the case. The leaders of the PNI received from the government a serious admonition to tread from now on the narrow path between the barely permissible and the proscribed.

The arbitrary actions of the police toward the popular meetings appear to be the order of the day. In Semarang, a propaganda meeting of the PNI was dispersed when Ir. Sukarno was reading a statement of principles of the PNI; this same statement and speech had been given more than thirty times without interference from the police. In Solo they left Ir. Sukarno very little freedom of speech. The police proscribed the use of the words *kemerdekaan* (freedom) and *pemerasaan* (exploitation), forbade him to say much, and warned that he would be prevented from speaking if he used words that did not please the police. The police terror, which we knew under the Fock regime and which led to underground activities, is emerging again under the "ethical" regime of Jonkheer de Graeff.

Thus the actions of the present governor-general are consistently at variance with the ethical policy, which he asserts to adhere to, and with his statement that he would not be a true Dutchman if he did not have respect for the nationalist ideals.

Thus far no trace has been apparent of this respect, flung as bait toward the Indonesian nationalists. What is the meaning of this respect when one cannot even use the word "freedom" at meetings. Moreover, this respect is very difficult to reconcile with the imperialist concept that Dutch supremacy in Indonesia should be maintained for an undetermined time. The ethical-coax-policy of Governor-General de Graeff is, in essence, ethical force.

As the highest servant of Dutch colonial imperialism, he cannot but be hostile toward the Indonesian nationalist movement. One is guilty of self-deceit, if one expects otherwise. But the Indonesian people, mindful of colonial history, which abounds in political hoaxes, will no longer be tricked. It becomes increasingly apparent that the colonial relationships remain dominated by irreconcilable conflicts of interest.

NOTES

1. From M. Hatta, *Verspreide Geschriften* pp. 537-548. The article, in Dutch, is entitled "Gouverneur General de Graeff en de Indonesische Vrijheidsbeweging," in *De Nieuwe Weg* (n.d.). Translated with permission of M. Hatta.
2. The original plan had been to have a native majority in the People's Council. The Feber Amendment (named after a member of the Dutch parliament) changed this in 1925. This caused considerable unhappiness among the Indonesians, and a committee comprised of some well-known cooperators, (M. H. Thamrin was chairman of the committee, R. A. A. A. Djajadiningrat was a

committee member) who sought to reverse the decision, was formed. In 1931 the change was effected, and the composition of the People's Council was thirty Indonesians, twenty-five Netherlanders, and three to five other Asians. S. L. van der Wali *De Volksraad en de Staatkundige Ontwikkeling van Nederlands-Indie* (Groningen: J. B. Wolters, 1965), II, p. 32.

Editor's Introduction:
The Round Table Conference

The Round Table Conference (RTC) was held in the Netherlands under the guidance of the United Nations to solve the Dutch-Indonesian conflict and to reach an agreement on the transfer of sovereignty to the republic, which had declared its independence on August 17, 1945.

Meetings started in August, 1949 and ended successfully in November. The republic ratified the RTC agreement on December 14 and the Netherlands on December 21. Formal transfer of sovereignty took place in Batavia, since then called Jakarta, on December 27, 1949.[1]

The plan to convene an RTC had come from the Netherlands. Relations between the two countries had steadily deteriorated after the Linggadjati Agreement had been signed in March, 1947. The Dutch twice had launched a military attack against the republic (July 1947 and December 1948), and twice the Indonesians had brought their plea before the United Nations Security Council.

With the last military action against the republic, the Dutch not only occupied Jogjakarta, the seat of the republican government, but they also arrested and exiled the Indonesian leaders. Their release was made a condition by the republican government before the resumption of talks. The Dutch at last relented. Adverse world opinion and allied pressure finally made the Dutch aware that their days as a colonial power were numbered.

The main issues at the RTC were the transfer of sovereignty, the settlement of the debt of the Netherlands Indies, the rights of minority groups outside the republican areas (that is, outside Java and Sumatra).

The Dutch yielded on the question of sovereignty, the Indonesians had to give in on other matters: they assumed the huge debt, including the cost of launching the two military attacks against the republic. The question of New Guinea was to be settled by a conference to be held within a year. However, not until January 1963 did New Guinea become part of the republic.

The Republic Indonesia Serikat created by the RTC was abrogated unilaterally by the Indonesians in August, 1950, and Indonesia became a unitary state.

Toward the Transfer of Sovereignty[2]

Now that we have gathered at this round table, each party should be motivated by the positive conviction that this conference should accomplish its goal here, to wit, the unconditional transfer of complete and real sovereignty to the Indonesian people. Then, at last, after four years of negotiations and fighting whereby a great deal was lost in lives and property, so sorely needed for the reconstruction of society and its production, one has come to realize that speedy conclusion of the present conflict is imperative. The bitter lessons experienced in the period now behind us demonstrated that the only solution to the Indonesian problem consists of the immediate transfer of sovereignty. The history of negotiations in the past has taught us that the crux of the difficulties lies in the question of sovereignty.

The sovereignty of the Netherlands over Indonesia is based upon history. But since the Indonesian declaration of independence of August 17, 1945, which was solemnly announced to the world as an expression of the right of the Indonesian people to decide their own fate, since then the Indonesian people have considered themselves sovereign.

The great change of attitude of the Indonesian people was in the beginning very difficult to understand for strangers who only knew the Indonesia of before the second world war. Not only the people in this country [the Netherlands] but also scholars and politicians, who should have been able to predict the future, were unable to understand that "the meekest people on earth" had become a rebellious people, driven by a dynamic spirit. One could not extricate oneself of the fallacious idea that the independence of Indonesia would only be a creation of a few demagogic leaders. One often neglected to make a thorough and serious analysis, which would have indicated that the proclamation of August 17, 1945 was the culmination of the Indonesian nationalist movement, which had been in existence for forty years. The unspeakably severe suffering under the Japanese domination merely strengthened the *mau merdeka* (the wish for independence).

As a result of this misunderstanding there developed, from the beginning, a psychological conflict between the Dutch people and the people of Indonesia, a conflict which became the source of the tragedy we have witnessed for four years. I call it a tragedy for, in essence, our goal is the same: namely, to grant Indonesia independence. There exist only differences of opinion in its implementation, and this has caused many clashes.

Regardless of the legal arguments the Netherlands government advances,[3] that the sovereignty over Indonesia rests with the Netherlands, the Indonesian people in the republic are of the opinion that their state is sovereign. They have their own government, not subjugated to another, they have their own army, and their own police force maintaining peace and law and order internally and externally, they have their own monetary system, and, last but not least, they also have their own foreign policy and foreign representation, which is expanding daily, establishing close relationships with other countries. All this is considered as so many indications of sovereignty which cannot simply be dismissed from the people's awareness. As time passed, the people became increasingly used to a life in freedom and sovereignty, and it became increasingly difficult to make independence disappear. Whether true or not, whether recognized or not, the Indonesian people in the republic consider themselves as living in a sovereign state. All the more because de facto authority of the Republic of Indonesia over Java, Madura, and Sumatra was already recognized after the signing of the Linggadjati Agreement,[4] not only by the Kingdom of the Netherlands, but also by the great powers such as England and the United States.

It is for that reason that every agreement already reached (such as the Linggadjati Agreement and the Renville principles) were, in its execution, invariably shipwrecked on the cliffs of solving the issue of sovereignty. In the opinion of the Dutch this sovereignty still rests completely in the hands of the Kingdom of the Netherlands, as long as this has not been transferred to the Indonesian people. The Indonesians believe that every transition period should represent a change from colonial status to a position of an independent state; therefore, the form of government in such a transitory stage should possess, as much as possible, the features of the government of the independent state. Thus . . . several rights and responsibilities could be transferred by the Netherlands to the provisional Indonesian government. To effectuate the independence of all of Indonesia via an interim period, the republic was willing to make sacrifices, namely, become a federal state rather than a sovereign state.

But it insisted that in such a case all the attributes of sovereignty, such as having an army and foreign relations should be taken over and continued by the interim government. In theory the sovereignty should rest with the Kingdom of the Netherlands during the interim period, but its practical execution, in many instances, would remain with the provisional government. The Indonesians believe that this concept is an agreement with the contents of the Renville principles[5] (Article 1 of the six additional articles).

This Indonesian plan gave rise to the problem of the allocation of responsibility between the Netherlands High Commissioner in Indonesia and the interim government, on which both parties failed to agree. And it is this problem of the allocation of responsibility, which halted all negotiations and twice evoked an armed conflict.

All this indicates that an interim period produces various problems, difficult to surmount, so that there is only one solution in settling the Indonesian question, namely, by transfer of sovereignty without an interim period.

If I am not mistaken, in Dutch political circles, in general, one has already accepted such a speedy transfer of sovereignty as unavoidable. And if this sovereignty will be transferred to the Indonesian people anyway, then it would be appropriate to expedite this transfer and to conclude the negotiations of the RTC, on this transfer, promptly.

The Indonesian-Dutch discord, in essence, is a psychological problem, originating in colonial history and additionally complicated by the four-year long psychological conflict. It is for that reason that every time lapse, which constitutes a postponement in granting sovereignty after an agreement has been reached, is felt by the Indonesian people as a political maneuver to maintain colonial power in Indonesia and thus the suspicion about Dutch intentions will increase. Lasting cooperation cannot be based on suspicion.

In the future the cooperation between Indonesia and the Netherlands can only endure if it is founded upon mutual understanding and trust. Our main goal, therefore, is directed toward the elimination of the feeling of distrust and the fortification of the desire to understand and collaborate. Thus everything that elicits distrust must be avoided.

Actually the transfer of sovereignty is not completely unconditional. We know that the Dutch government insists that the sovereignty be transferred to a federated Indonesia and that, between the Republic of Indonesia Serikat (Republic of the United States of Indonesia) and the

Kingdom of the Netherlands, a union will be formed in conformity with the Renville principles. Because the Indonesian side, the republic as well as the BFO,[6] agrees with the federal form and the establishment of a Netherlands-Indonesian Union these conditions are not considered to curtail sovereignty.

The republic has agreed, since the Linggadjati Agreement, to the formation of a federation, and recently this was confirmed in the decision of the Inter-Indonesian Conference. The union must be formed by two states, both sovereign, having an equal position in it. None of the two parties shall cede more rights to the union than the other. Thus we will acquire a union structure of a free association between two sovereign states. The prerequisite for this union is that it does not constitute an impediment for the complete and real sovereignty, which must be transferred to the Republic of Indonesia Serikat.

The concept of a union as a superstate, as was formerly advocated by the Dutch in Kaliurang,[7] had a great psychological effect on the Indonesian people and the suspicion arose that the Netherlands wanted to use the union to conceal the purpose preserving the "empire." It evokes satisfaction that the Dutch government and its delegation in Lake Success and in Djakarta have already repeatedly confirmed that the Netherlands does not seek the realization of a union in the form of a "superstate."

Because we are aware that this union question—in view of its history—greatly affects the psychology of the masses, we must observe caution in the establishment of its structure and the manner of its formation. This union must be voluntary, not rigid in structure and ties. For, if indeed the goal of that union is a close long-lasting cooperation between the Netherlands and Indonesia, it is necessary to make the structure flexible, or else this could in practice easily prompt reaction. Thus one would get further from the goal. If the union constitutes, in reality, a voluntary association between two states, both independent and equal, then each tight chain will break, because one would not adhere to it. And every regulation, which has become obsolete, is doomed to perish. It is actually harmful if a regulation is regarded as forced upon by one of the parties. A voluntary association cannot be imposed to secure a lasting collaboration; it should be accepted in complete freedom. Every bond considered binding will evoke counterforces, *in casu,* the urge to abrogate the union. Therefore in the formation of the union, wisdom and foresight are necessary so that the goal-content is not sacrificed to the structure-form.

I know that many in the Netherlands harbor fear that Netherlands capital and Netherlands economic interests will be imperiled when Indonesia becomes independent and sovereign. This fear advocates an attitude and policy which, looking into the past, aims to retain what should have been transferred, which led to a magnification of the psychological conflict. This contributed to the emergence of controversies ending in armed conflict, which was not the desired goal. The production, which should have been increased, was largely stopped; the means of production, which should have been preserved, were destroyed by the scorched-earth policy. Instead of directing forces toward production in the interest of the whole world which needs these goods and raw materials, they were geared toward destruction.

How good it would have been if, from the beginning, agreement had been reached on a transfer of sovereignty. The cooperation between Indonesia and the Netherlands would then already be a fact, the enlarged production would have begun and capital as well as other means of production would have been preserved.

But it makes little sense to discuss the course of past history, *Nasi telah mendjadi bubur* (no use crying over spilt milk). And as we know the state of mind in the past was such that all events were determined by their own psychological norms.

The fear that Dutch capital will be in danger in Indonesia if Indonesia becomes independent is totally without foundation. The Political Manifesto of the Government of the Republic Indonesia of November 1, 1945,[8] explicitly declared that these interests would be guaranteed. The paragraph in question states:

> We know and are well aware that in the years ahead in the interests of our country and our people we need, in the reconstruction of our country, help of strangers in the form of technicians and intellectuals as well as foreign capital.
>
> By the fulfillment of that need we shall not neglect to observe that persons, who speak Dutch, namely, the Dutch, will most likely be needed in much greater numbers, because they are already here and more accustomed to conditions in this country. Therefore the realization of our independence should not signify a great loss for the Netherlands, if measured by the capital or personnel employed, but it will naturally entail an enormous change in political status.
>
> We are convinced that our rich country, if developed in earnest to raise the standard of living of our people as well as of the world in general, could offer great opportunities for people all over the world, in particular from the United States of America, Australia, and the Philippines, to participate in the construction of our country and the elevation of our people. But this will only start when the dispute over sovereignty between us and the Netherlands is terminated with the recognition of our right to determine our own fate: namely, recognition of the state and form of government we ourselves have selected. Not only we, and perhaps the Netherlands too, have

an interest in its early implementation, but the whole world which awaits the contribution of Indonesia and its people in alleviating shortages existing in the world today.

With the recognition of our independence we shall assume our responsibility in conformity with our status. The whole debt of the Netherlands Indies of before the Japanese surrender, which is in all fairness ours, we shall recognize.

All foreign property except that needed for exploration by the state, will be returned to the rightful owners, with the understanding that a reasonable compensation will be given for that taken over by the state.

Thus far the position of the Government of the Republic has not changed.

The Netherlands should look ahead with the constructive idea that an independent and sovereign Indonesia will not be disadvantageous, but in the long run will be advantageous for the people of the Netherlands. In particular economic cooperation between Indonesia and the Netherlands should be regulated in such a way that the reconstruction of Indonesia can proceed according to a plan spanning decades, coordinated with the development of new industry in the Netherlands, which would supply Indonesia's needs for various goods and means of production.

Perhaps in one respect Dutch capital must indeed suffer a loss. The new system requires of the government a welfare policy for the people, which may result in future decrease of profits. . . . Independent Indonesia will no longer be the *inlanderkolonie* of former days,[9] providing coolies at low wages. The new independent Indonesia will demand a living wage and social security for all workers, recognized in all civilized countries in conformity with the fourth of the freedoms advanced by the late President Roosevelt, namely, "freedom from want." But a prosperous Indonesia with greater purchasing power, in the long run, will not signify a loss for the outside world and, in particular, not for the Netherlands; on the contrary, it will mean gain.

The transfer of sovereignty by the Kingdom of the Netherlands to the Republic Indonesia Serikat will go hand-in-hand with the transfer of debts and claims, rights and duties. And therefore this will be an item on the agenda of the Round Table Conference. We can already expect that this question will show many difficult aspects and that there will be numerous problems of detail. The solution of these, according to me, should not prolong the duration. . . . We must confine the discussion to the main problems and principles so that the Round Table Conference can be rapidly concluded and will not last longer than is psychologically justified. Details between the Netherlands and the Republic of Indonesia Serikat can be agreed upon later.

January 1, 1949,[10] the date which had such great effect on the psyche of the Indonesian people, now lies far behind us. All considerations are now directed toward the year 1949. The transfer of sovereignty to the Indonesian people must be settled in this very year. Before the year 1950 begins Indonesia must be independent, the Republic Indonesia Serikat must have been established, equipped with total and true sovereignty. This is a demand of mass psychology, which we must not disregard. A question of irrationality perhaps, but it may not be neglected!

Mr. Chairman! I believe that, if we, conferring at this round table, conduct our deliberations in earnest, want to find a solution for the Indonesian question in the form of an unconditional surrender of the complete and real sovereignty, we should direct our full attention to the future of both our peoples. If our attention is indeed directed toward that goal, then, I am confident, the differences of opinion will be small and the purpose of this Round Table Conference will be quickly accomplished.

For four years our peoples have lived in mutual animosity and with feelings of hate in our hearts. For four years we have fought and murdered each other, with futile sacrifice of property and people.

Let us now start a new history, founded upon peace and cooperation; thereby the Indonesian and the Dutch people will share in prosperity. Our children and our grandchildren, the future generations, will be grateful to us.

May God the Almighty bestow His blessing on our work at the Round Table Conference.

NOTES

1. Alastair M. Taylor, *Indonesian Independence and the United Nations* (Ithaca: Cornell University Press, 1960), pp. 227-264.
2. From M. Hatta, *Verspreide Geschriften,* pp. 316-323. Speech at the opening of the Round Table Conference, August, 1949. Dutch title: "Naar de Souvereiniteits overdracht." Translated with permission of M. Hatta.
3. The Netherlands insisted that they had sovereignty over the islands of the archipelago and that the republic could not unilaterally abrogate this right.
4. With the signing of the Linggadjati Agreement (March, 1947), the Netherlands acknowledged the de facto authority of the republic over Java, Madura, and Sumatra.
5. The Renville principles, named after the U.S. Navy ship placed at the disposal of the negotiating parties, the republic and the Netherlands, under the aegis of the United Commission of Good Offices. This commission was instrumental in securing an acceptance of basic principles which would constitute a foundation for further negotiations. The principles were vague, and one of the stipulations was that a plebiscite would determine which areas wanted to form part of the republic. Boundaries were also redrawn to the detriment of the republic. Allied pressure forced the republic to agree to these principles.

6. BFO, Bijeenkomst Federaal Overleg, in English Assembly for Federal Consultation. A series of conferences held under the aegis of the Netherlands between several ethnic groups not belonging to the republic. The intention was to come to a federated Indonesia, but the republic was not a participating party and the object was clearly the creation of a series of Dutch puppet states. George McTurnan Kahin, *Nationalism and Revolution in Indonesia* (Ithaca: Cornell University Press, 1952), pp. 386–387, 408–414.
7. Resort near Jogjakarta, where some of the preliminary meetings of the Renville conference were held.
8. Political Manifesto was written by Sutan Sjahrir.
9. Inlander kolonie, native colony. Although the word *inlander* means native, it had acquired a derogatory connotation over the years, and its use was greatly disliked by the Indonesians.
10. January 1, 1949 was the date stipulated in the Linggadjati Agreement for the formation of the Dutch Indonesian Union and the establishment of the federated Indonesian state.

Ir. Sukarno

Ir. Sukarno: Unifier of a Thousand Islands[1]
(1901-1970)

Sukarno was born in Surabaya on June 6, 1901 which made him a Gemini; this—as he himself explained—accounted for his apparent dual personality.[2] His father was a teacher belonging to the low Javanese nobility, his mother was a dancer and a member of a Balinese Brahmin caste.

Sukarno attended a Dutch grade school and high school in Surabaya, where he became acquainted with socialism through one of his Dutch teachers and with the nationalist movement through his landlord H. O. S. Tjokroaminoto, at the time the leader of the Sarekat Islam. After graduating from high school, Sukarno enrolled at the newly opened technical college in Bandung and launched his political career by establishing the Bandung Study Club. Although he acquired a title (Ir., engineer), he made little use of his technical training as architect and engineer.

In 1927 the Perserikatan Indonesia was launched (the name was later changed, in 1928, to Partai Nasional Indonesia); its goal was Indonesian independence to be accomplished by fostering awareness among the Indonesian people and by seeking cooperation with other organizations having a similar goal. The arrest of four Indonesian students in the Netherlands (among them M. Hatta), marked the start of a vehement anticolonial campaign. Sukarno's militance and widespread popular appeal brought admonition from the government, eventually resulting in his arrest and conviction. Despite a brilliant plea in his own defense entitled *Indonesia Accuses,* a scathing attack on colonialism, he was sentenced to four years in prison, but Governor-General de Graeff pardoned him in 1931. For a while Sukarno led another party, but resigned in 1933 purportedly because he had become aware of the futility of noncooperation. He was arrested again in 1933 (in Thamrin's home), later exiled to Flores, and in 1938 to Benkulen in Sumatra. In 1941 he rejected a Dutch offer to liberate him in exchange for serving the colonial cause in the looming conflict with Japan and instead waited for the Japanese to return him to Java (1942).

During the Japanese occupation Sukarno again rose to national prominence and the sudden end of the Pacific war was seized upon by him and Hatta to proclaim Indonesia's independence. But it was not until December, 1949 that Dutch sovereignty over Indonesia was transferred to the Indonesian people. Sukarno became Indonesia's first president and remained in that position until 1966. His alleged implication in the abortive communist coup of 1965 led to his fall from power. He was ailing and living in seclusion, when he died in 1970.

Sukarno's significance in the fight for independence and unity must not be underestimated. In the nineteen twenties he sought to foster awareness in the people's minds and instill in them a sense of pride in their national heritage and history. He unfailingly advocated unity despite diversity among the different ethnic groups of the archipelago and was instrumental in creating the unitary state Indonesia is now. Sukarno should be assessed for these positive and great contributions to present-day Indonesia.

NOTES

1. Several studies in English have appeared on Sukarno, and I would like to single out one. Bernhard Dahm, *Sukarno and the Struggle for Indonesian Independence,* trans. by Mary F. Somers Heidhues (Ithaca: Cornell University Press, 1969), gives a good analysis of Sukarno's political thinking and in particular provides a comprehensive background of the Indonesian nationalist movement.
2. *Sukarno: An Autobiography as Told to Cindy Adams* (New York: Bobbs Merrill Company, 1965) gives an interesting personal account.

Toward a Brown Front[1]

Zentgraaf of the *Soerabaiaasch Handelsblad* at one time advocated the forming of a white front[2] to forcefully withstand the mass of *inlanders,* who in their various organizations were steadily gaining terrain at the expense of the prestige of the whites, which in the past was extensive enough to protect the alien ruler against the "murderousness" and the "bloodthirstiness" of the Indigenous.

His call has remained unheeded. It did not encounter positive reaction in the white press in this country. It elicited only a negative reply from the *sana* party: one rejected the idea of a white front.

We can interpret this attitude of the press in two ways. We can say that the white man really wants to work toward fraternization, toward mutual appreciation between brown and white. Perhaps we can explain this attitude by declaring that . . . the formation and consolidation of a white front will tend to weaken the white front and will irrevocably provoke a brown front whereby the brown man could, with the weight of his numbers, tip the scales which could not be offset by the organizational strength of the white man alone.

Which of the two explanations is the most plausible? Against the first explanation can be advanced that, in the past, one has never felt the need for fraternization.

The white man in our country has carefully isolated himself; he has isolated himself from everything that was not "white," he rejected every approach from our side; he established a society that had no points of contact with the Indonesian. Why then suddenly this *liebaugeln?* Why these ideas of fraternization?

We, Indonesians, we consider this suspect?

For the second hypothesis pleads the fact that one exudes fraternal love just at the time when we Indonesians have secured strength through power-formation in several organizations; that at present we do not merely constitute a mass of illiterates but a mass of organized illiterates, and we know that what we lack in scholastic wisdom, organizational talent, and technique is amply compensated by our numbers.

Certainly, we Indonesians understand that now we have grown increasingly conscious of our power based upon our numerical majority, coupled with the ever-decreasing prestige of the alien ruler, the relationship will become increasingly acerbated. We understand that the mathematical demarcation of the boundaries between power-desiring brown and power-clinging white means the emergence of the climax of the deteriorating relationship between white and brown. But we also understand that the clearer and the sooner the antithesis is posed, the more meaningful the struggle will be; and that the clearer the antagonism is recognized the more precise the purpose of the struggle will be.

When we realize this, then the next step we Indonesians should take is obvious.

Assuming that we are ready to accept all that is reasonable and adopt this as our own; that we must be ready to accept lessons even from our adversaries, albeit amended in conformity with our interests—then we should follow the advice of Zentgraaf.

A "white front" weakens the European position in our country. Thus, we can infer that obviously a "brown front" will strengthen our position!

What the opponent rejects must therefore naturally be advantageous to us. We should proceed toward power alignment, toward a consolidation which only realistic policies can effectuate, toward a consolidation of power which is only possible with the formation of a "brown front."

Therefore let the brown front come! So that every Indonesian may recognize that lack of unity has been the cause of our defeats in our struggles with the west. That he may learn from history of our national decline, from the court intrigues of the Mangkurats, or from the struggle during Mangkubumi and Mas Said,[3] from which not the Indonesians but only the Dutch emerged victorious. . . .

Not with thousands and thousands of *inlanders* the foreigner must have to deal; not with millions of browns should he have to struggle; he should have confronting him one, inseparable Indonesian people—wellnigh one, inseparable Indonesian nation!

How can this be, when in reality our people are divided into so many organizations? How can this be when those organizations all have their own ideology and all follow their own method of fighting?

In the first place, one should be warned against making an effort to bring about unification of the various parties. One must be convinced of the impossibility to tie in the trammels of one single organization, a nation of fifty million souls, living in a many faceted societal structure; and, if this were possible, would force upon Indonesia a stamp of ideas—and a poverty of mind, which excludes a free, independent existence and thus would condemn our nation to carry the yoke of slavery until doomsday.

And thus federation should be our slogan. Federation, which should leave intact the personality, the individuality, the character of the joined parties. And the tie, indispensable for holding the parties together, should be very loose. It should be like the loose tie binding the parts of the British empire. It should be loose in order to be tight.

The agreement to be made by the Indonesian parties, therefore, cannot be an agreement on principles. Agreement on principles implies subjugation to discipline of the joined; this means certain sacrifice of independence and freedom of movement of the joined parties.

And an alliance without party discipline, without sacrifice of freedom, without sacrifice of the independence of the joined parties in the interest of the alliance itself—such a union is feasible. Yes, such a union is feasible when one is satisfied with incidental cooperation, cooperation only then when the affiliated unanimously feel the urgency for this. Cooperation for instance on the right of assembly. Cooperation on the penal sanction.[4] Cooperation on the mass arrests or the exorbitant powers. Cooperation on our student martyrs in Holland. . . .[5] We Indonesians, we should be ashamed that over and over again our attacks on the penal sanction or sugar capital are successfully repulsed. . . . We should be ashamed that after the first reports of student raids or arrests not one of us has packed his suitcases to secure further details firsthand; that up to now we are not able to give the movement the element of strength.

May, therefore, the Permufakatan Partij Partij Politiek Indonesia soon be born.[6] So that we, aware of our difficult task, may seek strength in each other to form an inseparable nation, to create a free sovereign community of independents. So that we soon may solder together the iron chain of the brown front!

Let our number be One!

NOTES

1. From *Dibawah Bendera Revolusi, Vol. 1,* K. Gunadi and H. M. Nasution, eds. (Djakarta: Panitia Penerbit Dibawah Bendera Revolusi, 1959) pp. 37–40. Originally published as "Naar het Bruine Front," in *Suluh Indonesia Mudah,* (1927). Apparently this is the only article Sukarno ever wrote in Dutch.

2. H. C. Zentgraaf, a conservative and very unscrupulous Dutch journalist.
3. Mangkurats-Amangkurats, rulers of Mataram in the seventeen and eighteen centuries; Mangkubumi-Hamengku Buwono rulers over Jogjakarta. The succession struggle in Mataram and the intervention the rulers sought of the Netherlanders gradually brought large parts of Java under the domination of the East India Company.
4. Penal sanction. Clause in the labor contract of the plantation coolie prohibiting the breaking of the contract by the laborer. See p. 73, herein.
5. Referring to the arrest of the four students of the Perhimpunan Indonesia in the Netherlands. See p. 129, herein.
6. Permufakatan Perhimpunan-Perhimpunan Politiek Kebangsaan Indonesia was founded in 1927. Abbreviated as PPPKI.

Can Noncooperation Not Bring About Mass Action and Power Formation?[1]

At present there are three movements among the Indonesian radicals.

One movement wants only noncooperation for the councils existing in Indonesia; one movement wants noncooperation for all the representative bodies of the dominating power, which is my view, as I have explained in previous articles; and then there is another movement which rejects this noncooperation altogether.

This last doctrine is advocated by one of the radicals who is still in Europe. One of the objections he advanced against this noncooperation is that this noncooperation does not bring about mass action and power formation.

Are these objections valid?

These objections are totally fallacious! For what are the facts?

The facts indicate that this noncooperation, such as is found in Hindustan [British India], can stimulate mass action which causes the body of the whole nation to tremble and can inspire the soul of the people, which according to Henriette Roland Holst,[2] is without equal in this world, as is apparent from the organization of Congress (a political organization opposing British rule in India in the twenties and thirties), which formed a variety of resistance groups in their attack against the enemy.

The facts indicate that noncooperation in Ireland, in the years 1916-1920, did bring about mass action which shook the whole body of the nation and was able to form a mighty concentration of power.

The facts indicate also that noncooperation in other countries, for example, Hungary, Korea, and others can also bring about this mass action and power formation.

The facts indicate also that noncooperation in our country—advocated by the PNI, PSI, Partindo, Pendidikan Nasional Indonesia, and earlier also by PKI and SR—can ignite mass action and power formation although mass action and power formation here are not comparable to mass action and power formation in Hindustan or Ireland.

And if the movement in Hindustan has until now not yielded a hundred percent result, if the Hindustani movement has until now not brought about an independent Hindustan, if the Hindustan movement has sometimes "become cold," this is not the fault of noncooperation, but it is the fault of the way in which noncooperation is carried out. Indian noncooperation is in my opinion too passive a form of noncooperation, which lacks aggression, lacks pressure, lacks attack, and lacks militancy. Indian noncooperation is characterized by what Gandhi himself called "passive civil disobedience." Jawaharlal Nehru and even Sen Gupta, who are known to be *lunak* [soft], once asked Gandhi if this passive civil disobedience can become militant civil-disobedience.

But because Gandhi based his noncooperation on the teachings of *ahimsa,* which prohibits any kind of aggression, Gandhi staunchly defended this stand. In my opinion this appears to be the reason the noncooperation movement in India is afflicted with "becoming cold."

This is why the uninformed public often has asked whether with noncooperation the Hindustani people can achieve a free India.

Our noncooperation is not based on the belief of *ahimsa,* it is not based on the doctrine of "do not oppose the evil," and does not rely on the doctrine of avoiding and not attacking those who are evil; because our noncooperation, as I have explained in previous articles, is based on the belief and the fact that between *sana* and *sini,* there is a conflict of interests which cannot be surmounted or bridged. Our noncooperation is, as I have explained, imbued with activity and radicalism—radicalism of spirit, radicalism of thought, radicalism in behavior, radicalism in every attitude, overt and covert. This radicalism rejects a passive position, this radicalism does not recognize the position "only wait, do not attack," this radicalism pursues a militant course. We must not adopt the position only wait, do not attack, we must get out of our houses, go outside to carry out the offensive against all of the enemy's strongholds.

And how about Ireland? In Ireland the people's movement became indeed "cold" as soon as noncooperation was no longer consistently pursued. The Irish people, who under the banner of noncooperation could not be subjugated, could not be defeated, could not have their movement broken, even though England sent guns, cannons, and tanks, and yes, even when England formed shock troops called Black and Tans—the Irish mass action and power formation experienced a setback when some groups who at first where militant noncooperators became meek and preferred to collaborate with England.

Naturally, the people's struggle in the independent countries, countries which have a national parliament, such as England, France, Germany, Belgium, and the Netherlands, the struggle of the people there became mighty and strong and erupted concurrently with parliamentary fights. Certainly parliamentary elections in particular provide an effective goal, a point of departure, a means for agitation and mass action. Of course it is a great mistake if in these free countries the struggle for parliamentary seats and the fights accompanying parliamentary action is not used as a tool for propaganda and a means for spirited action.

If Indonesia had a national parliament as has Germany, or France, or England, or Belgium, or the Netherlands, we certainly would not be averse to stimulate mass action and to consolidate power in the fight for parliamentary seats and the struggle which accompanies parliamentary action.

But as long as at the apex of our country is entrenched a master country; as long as the *sana* group is sitting on the *sini*'s neck, we need to enlarge and to widen the gap between *sana* and *sini;* and as long as Indonesia is stigmatized with the name Netherlands Indies and is not yet named Indonesia *Merdeka,* we must always adhere to noncooperation as the basis of our struggle. For noncooperation in a colonized country will never freeze mass action and weaken power formation, on the contrary, it will spur mass action and strengthen the consolidation of power.

What is this mass action? On this subject, even within the movement itself, some people still misunderstand mass action. They believe that "mass action" is something that will happen later. They say that what we are doing now is only preparation which will lead to mass action. "Get ready now, get organized now, get prepared now for everything—and then later, like waves of a flood breaking open the dikes, mass action will start," that is what some people think.

Such a concept is totally wrong. But sometimes this kind of thinking also exists within the nationalist movement. This concept is sometimes found especially among people who confuse the word *massa* [masses] with *masa* [time]. Such a notion was also present in the thinking of the "wily" presiding judge of the *landraad,* who at the time of my trial said: "P.N.I. is busy making preparations, its mass action will occur later when preparations are completed."

Therefore, it is of primary importance to us to answer the question: What constitutes mass action?

Mass action is action of the masses. And the masses are: all those millions of Marhaens.[3] Thus mass action is the action of all those millions of Marhaens. And action means performance, movement, struggle of those millions of Marhaens. And this performance, movement, struggle is not something that will take place later; this performance, this movement, this struggle is what we are pursuing now. The things we do now, the actions we take, all those steps we take today—such as organizing a club, writing articles in journals or newpapers, organizing lectures and seminars, public meetings, demonstrations—all of these constitute performance, movement, and struggle of those millions of Marhaens, all of these constitute mass action.

Thus mass action is not some future phenomenon, not something that has not yet happened, not a flood which will free us in the future, but mass action is a current issue. Everyday now we can see mass action. Mass action exists already in the activity of the organizations, and organization is already contained in the activities of this mass action. "In the organization the action is already contained and in the action, the organization," thus spoke August Bebel correctly and concisely,[4] although mass action need not be and is not always a movement of the organized common people. The history of the world has seen several cases of success without organization. World history, for instance, has seen mass action of the "common people" in the French Revolution, mass action of the Belgian people in the year 1830 against Dutch authority, and mass action of the tea coolies in Gandhi's movement. These are examples of mass action which, without organization, suddenly occurred and took their own course, drawing its strength from society, which was static but suddenly awoke to become dynamic.

But it can be truly said that what we are pursuing now is mass action. And if our movement at present has not sufficient intensity, if our movement now is not one-hundred percent active, if our movement is not like a flood bursting through the dikes, it is not because we have not espoused mass action, but because our mass action has not yet reached its zenith.

Is not such an explanation of the meaning of mass action sufficient? Is the explanation that this mass action is the movement of the millions of Marhaens enough? Such an explanation does not suffice at all. Because our statement does not include yet another aspect which is very important in the issue of mass action. Our statement has failed to explain that mass action must be imbued with radical spirit and activity, with revolutionary spirit and activity.

Not every movement of the common people constitutes mass action. Not every movement having hundreds, thousands, millions of people constitutes mass action. Mass action is a radical and revolutionary movement of millions of common people. A movement of the common people which is not radical and revolutionary, a movement of the common people which is not imbued with spiritual resistance, a movement of the common people which is not fierce and imbued with a spirit of a *banteng,* such a movement of the common people, even if these millions of people are active, does not constitute mass action but only *Massale actie,* or action on a grand scale.

In my previous analysis I explained what can be called mass action. I directed the attention of the reader especially to the important question relating to the understanding of mass action. Mass action must be radical and revolutionary; mass action which is not imbued with spiritual resistance, mass action which is not imbued with the spirit of a *banteng,* such mass action is not truly mass action, but it is only *Massale actie*—this is what I said.

Naturally this radical and revolutionary aspect "stigmatizes" mass action in *technisch-politieke term*—a political term which cannot be translated into Indonesian. Of course this radical and revolutionary aspect distinguishes mass action from the popular "movement of the common people." See, for instance, the Indonesian popular movement in the past, when the Sarekat Islam appeared. . . .

A thousand, ten thousand, a hundred thousand, yes, a million people are active together—a million people are in action together—but their action is only *Massale actie* and not mass action, because their action is not radical and revolutionary.

Consider also this funny phenomenon: people sometimes write in the newspaper that this or that party on a particular day organized a mass action to protest a certain situation, as if mass action is an occurrence of that particular day, as if mass action is a matter that can be ordered or stopped at a specific hour. No! Mass action is not a matter "of a particular day," mass action is not a matter which can be "cabled" to start this hour and be terminated at that hour—mass action is the awakening of the radical and revolutionary masses brought about by forces within the society itself. Mass action is a revolutionary movement which is self-generated; and when people report that this or that party on a particular day will organize mass action, it actually means . . . that several meetings are held simultaneously! . . .

Now can noncooperation indeed promote genuine mass action? Noncooperation can indeed intensify mass action, that is, a mass movement imbued with radicalism. As I explained earlier, noncooperation, in particular, in the struggle in a colonial country, is imbued with radicalism. In the realm of national politics various tactical struggles have been employed to fight imperialism: some are *non-,* some are *co-,* some are not *non-,* or some are not *co-,* but there is only one which is basically and fundamentally radical and revolutionary, that is the course of noncooperation. Because only noncooperation, which consciously and fundamentally pursues the antithesis between *sana* and *sini,* acknowledges its existence and pursues this fact, thus widens the gap between *sana* and *sini.*

But this is not all! Noncooperation, because it stimulates this antithesis, is the only basic strategy in a colonized country which, according to the writer who calls himself a revolutionary politician in the newspaper *Utusan Indonesia,* can infuse the struggle with revolutionary zeal, that is, with revolutionary charge.

Noncooperation, which can infuse revolutionary zeal, provides an essential ingredient in the issue of mass action; revolutionary zeal can prompt popular movements to adopt mass action. . . .

The fighting procedure in free countries make parliamentary elections and the fights within parliament a starting point, forum, or command post for the public struggle, as I explained in a previous article. This method of fighting cannot be employed effectively in a colonized country, especially not in a colony like Indonesia. Neither the elections-seats-representative council procedure nor the forum provided by the council, neither the opportunity to make the council a command post, nor the opportunity to expose the enemy's hypocrisy—all these in a colonized country like Indonesia are merely cheap trickery and are only a phoney shadow of the elections-seats-parliamentary procedure of the free countries, of the parliamentary forum of the free countries, the command post of the free countries.

How could we stimulate mass action with elections-seats-representative councils, if the elections-seats-representative councils do not provide for representation of the people and are completely manipulated by the BB and governmental bodies alone? How can we make the representative bodies a forum for mass action, if the usage of a word such as *overheerser* is considered *tabu* and proscribed? How could we make the council a command post of mass action, when, for instance, a meek speech delivered by Mr. Otto [Oto] Iskander Dinata recently caused the president's gavel to dance on the table as if seized by the devil?[5]

No! The opportunity to make the representative council a starting point, a forum, a command post for our struggle is not at all analogous with the opportunity provided by the parliaments of the free nations . . . . it is only a mere "photograph of the back"!

Thus if we radicals, in a colonized country like Indonesia, want to awaken and arouse mass action on a large scale, we must pursue a direction which will not render the distorted view of the "photograph of the back," but pursue a policy of noncooperation determinedly and irrevocably.

I shall again explain the question of the relationship between noncooperation and the formation of power.

In my previous analysis I explained that, in the world of politics in a colonized country, noncoooperation is the only basic course of resistance which can produce mass action.

Now we must clarify how noncooperation can also bring about the formation of power. What is power formation? This is a very important question. Just as we cannot answer the question of noncooperation in relationship to mass action, before we can answer what mass action is, similarly we cannot discuss the formation of power before we understand what power formation is (just as talking about mass action often becomes idle chatter, when there is no notion of what is being discussed).

Once again what is this power formation? Power formation means creating power. Power formation is the only way to force the *sana* to follow our wishes. This force is necessary, is a prerequisite.

Listen to what I said recently when I presented my defense:[6]

> Power formation, the forming of power because the colonial issue is the issue of authority, the issue of power. Power formation, because throughout world history it is shown that great change only takes place by those who are victorious... .No class will ever voluntarily relinquish its right, thus spoke Marx. As long as the Indonesian people do not possess supreme power, as long as the Indonesian people are divided and are not working in harmony, as long as our people cannot press their demands backed by an organized and consolidated power—until then the imperialist power will continue to pursue its own interests and regard them [the Indonesian people] as docile sheep and will continue to ignore their demands. Because every demand of the Indonesian people is disadvantageous to imperialism, no demand of the Indonesian people will be met unless imperialism is forced to grant it. Every victory of the Indonesian people over imperialism and colonial government is the result of pressure the people have exerted. Every gain of the Indonesian people is an extorted concession.[7]

These are the sentences from my book.

Therefore once again power formation is consolidation of power needed to exert pressure upon the *sana*. Power formation is imperative because of the existing conflict of interests between *sana* and *sini*—all our demands are opposed to the *sana*'s demands, collide with the *sana*'s interests, are harmful to the *sanas*—and until the *sana* will yield to our demands, we must back up our demands with pressure that they cannot contain.

We can only exert pressure for those demands when we have energy, power, authority, *MACHT;* therefore, we must consolidate power, that is, work to consolidate power with energy and diligence.

Power formation is a matter based on the antithesis between *sana* and *sini,* a matter supported by spiritual resistance and the belief that there can be no peace between *sana* and *sini.* . . .

Just as surely as radicalism is the crux of mass action, so is radicalism the focal point of power formation. Power formation without radicalism, power formation without the principle of antithesis and resistance, such power formation is not genuine.

People can initiate extensive membership drives, people can set up many different organizations; people can establish many cooperative bodies, many trade unions, many schools; can start a variety of magazines, a variety of activities, but all of these will only lead to a consciousness and subservience of a goat; unless all of these activities are imbued with radical and revolutionary fervor, they cannot be called power formation or the creation of power.

Because as I explained before, this concept of power formation leads to the antithesis between *sana* and *sini,* to the total opposition between *sana* and *sini.*

Let us, for example, once more take the Sarekat Islam of the past. It had many members, many branches, many cooperatives, many trade unions, a great deal of everything, but because their ideas and activites were directed toward peace, it could not be considered directed toward the formation of power and naturally was not feared by the enemy. Let us take another example: Partai Nasional Indonesia. Spiritual and actual radicalism exist, is organized, and will organize its strength toward the backbone of imperialism. That party was greatly feared by the enemy and was crushed before the power formation expanded![8] Naturally it was the only party in Indonesia which organized genuine formation of power.

Now can noncooperation bring about the formation of power? As in a colonized country, noncooperation provides the means in its struggle to ignite mass action, so in a colonized country it is the only course which can stimulate the people's power formation. Because, as the readers already know, only noncooperation acknowledges the existence and deepens the antithesis and the struggle between *sana* and *sini.*

Noncooperation and power formation, which are both imbued with spiritual and actual radicalism, are mutually interrelated, support each other, and strengthen each other.

Therefore, whoever wishes the formation of power in Indonesia must embrace noncooperation.

NOTES

1. From *Dibawah Bendera Revolusi,* pp. 193–202. Originally "Noncooperation tidak bisa mendatangkan massa-aksi dan machtsvorming?" in *Fikiran Ra'jat,*

2.	(1932-1933). The greater part of this article was translated by Mr. Peter Anada, Southeast Asia Bibliographer, University of California at Berkeley.
2.	Henriette Roland Holst-van der Schalk, Dutch writer and well-known socialist (1869-1952).
3.	Marhaen, the common people. Sukarno relates the story of how he adopted the use of this name. During a walk one day he met a rice farmer who worked in his own field using his own tools but who was evidently not a proletarian. When Sukarno asked him his name he replied: Marhaen. Sukarno then decided to use this name to depict the suffering people of Indonesia. See: B. Dahm, *Sukarno and the Struggle,* p. 143.
4.	August Bebel, German Social Democrat (1840-1913).
5.	Oto Iskander Dinata, was a member of the People's Council from 1931-1942. He was the chairman of Pasundan, a political party that sought to advance the interests of the Sundanese people (in West Java).
6.	At his trial in 1930 Sukarno presented a plea in his own defense: *Indonesia Menggugat* [Indonesia accuses!].
7.	Meaning concession. If the enemy, because of our pressure, yields to some or all of our demands then the enemy is making concessions. (This is Sukarno's note.)
8.	When this party was formed, the boom was immediately lowered. (This is Sukarno's note.)

L. N. Palar. Photograph courtesy of the Permanent Mission of the Republic of Indonesia to the United Nations.

L. N. Palar: Socialist and Diplomat
(Born 1902)

By Royal Decree of May 31, 1946, Lambertus Nicodemus Palar became a member of the lower house of the Dutch parliament of the Kingdom of the Netherlands.[1] He took his seat on June 6, the day after his forty-fourth birthday. Palar was not the first Indonesian to join the Dutch parliament; Rustam Effendi, affiliated with the Communist party, had preceeded him in the nineteen thirties.

Palar was born in Menado, an area in Northern Sulawesi with a predominantly Christian population regarded by the colonial rulers as one of the most loyal in the archipelago. Palar went to school in Indonesia, worked for a short while in the Indies' largest shipping company, then departed for the Netherlands in the late twenties.

He enrolled as a student at the University of Amsterdam, at that time the most left-wing institution of higher education in the Netherlands, and quickly came under the influence of socialism. From 1933 to 1939 he worked simultaneously for the Social Democratic party, the socialist labor union, and *Persindo* the news agency that sought to disseminate socialist principles to the Indonesian press. His collaborator was the former People's Council member J. E. Stokvis.

In the prewar years Palar wrote several articles on major issues confronting the Indonesian nationalist movement which were published in socialist journals. The tone of all his writings is moderate, the message clear and invariably free of invective.

From December 1938 to June 1939 Palar undertook a study trip through the archipelago on behalf of the Socialist party. He recorded his impressions of meetings with the nationalist leaders in an article in which he warned of the dangers of the pursued colonial policy and the attraction Japan and its policies had for the nationalists. But his readership consisted primarily of liberal left-of-the-center intellectuals, both in the Netherlands and in the Indies, who had no say in shaping colonial policy.[2]

From 1945 to 1947 Palar was a board member of the Party of Labor and an editor of its daily newspaper. This party was a descendant of the prewar Social Democratic party without its Marxist base, and subsequently lost much of its militancy. Palar served this party in parliament from June 1946 until July 1947, making a total of five speeches all concerning Indonesia. He was a loyal party member; thus he voted against a Communist party member's amendment to prohibit shipment of troops to Indonesia, arguing that, if these shipments were illegal they would be so designated by the negotiators in Batavia.[3]

Palar visited Indonesia in April and May of 1947, a trip which appears to have influenced him greatly and convinced him that the republic was indeed viable and had widespread and considerable support in the archipelago.

Palar's speech reprinted here is an eloquent and impartial plea for reason, an attempt to present the opinion of his fellow countrymen but also an effort to understand the Dutch point of view. Yet between the lines one can read an account of Dutch deviousness and wily schemes seeking to annihilate the republic and thus maintain a firm foothold in Indonesia.

But Palar pleaded in vain, and he resigned his seat the day after the Dutch "police action" against the republic commenced, because he regarded this, and rightly so, as but a calculated, full-scale military attack for the purpose of destroying its government.

From the Tweede Kamer, Palar moved to the United Nations, and in 1950 became Indonesia's first ambassador to this organization. He subsequently filled several ambassadorial posts: the German Federal Republic, India, the U.S.S.R. and Canada. In 1962 he returned to his former post at the U.N.; he later took Indonesia out of the world organization at Sukarno's orders and after the latter's fall from power returned it to the U.N.'s fold.

Palar resigned from the diplomatic service in 1968 and is now living in Jakarta.

NOTES

1. The Netherlands have an election system of proportional representation. A party is allocated seats in parliament in proportion to the votes it has received in the country at large.

Thus one does not vote for a person but for the party. By election time the party makes up a list of candidates and from this list of names the party's representatives for parliament are selected.
2. Articles written by L. N. Palar, "Over Boven Digoel," *Socialistische Gids* (1938), pp. 306–312; "De Indonesische Beweging en Japan," *Socialisme en Democratie* (1939), pp. 793–805; "De Indonesische Nationale Beweging," *Leven en Werken* (1939), pp. 359–372.
3. Kingdom of the Netherlands, Staten Generaal, Tweede Kamer, *Handelingen 1946/47,* September 25, 1946, p. 53.

Editor's Introduction:
The Linggadjati Agreement[1]

The sudden Japanese surrender on August 15, 1945 provided the Indonesians with an opportunity to declare their independence (August 17). When the British arrived in Java on September 29, they found a working administration that appeared quite capable of maintaining law and order. In any case, the limited British forces would have been unable to wage a war against the republic.

Thus, when the Netherlands Indies government returned from exile in Australia in November (all Dutch civilians had been interned for the duration of the Japanese occupation), their intention to regain the islands by force was thwarted by the British military authorities, who had recognized the Indonesian republic de facto and who had refused to become embroiled in a colonial war. Allied pressure forced the Dutch to negotiate with the republic, but relations between the Dutch and Indonesians continued to deteriorate, in particular, when the Dutch commenced troop landings in February 1946.

In September 1946 the Dutch parliament (which had a Catholic-Labor majority) appointed a commission under the chairmanship of Professor Schermerhorn (a liberal member of the Labor party), who with other commission members, seemed genuinely interested in terminating the Indonesian impasse and coming to an agreement with the republic. Negotiations started in November in Linggadjati West Java, under the aegis of Lord Killearn, special British envoy for Southeast Asia. The chief negotiator for the Indonesian side was Sutan Sjahrir.

The agreement was approved by the Dutch parliament in December, but gradually the goodwill in the Netherlands that was prevalent when the commission was appointed vanished. Vociferous Dutch groups started a denunciatory campaign directed against the commission members and the lieutenant governor-general. Even before the agreement was signed it became apparent that it no longer had the support of the cabinet.

The Linggadjati Agreement was signed by both parties in Batavia on March

25, 1946. Its main provisions were: the Netherlands recognized the *de facto* authority of the republic over Java, Madura, and Sumatra; a federal state would be established consisting of the republic and other states in the archipelago, together forming the United States of Indonesia—a Netherlands Indonesian Union would be formed consisting of the Netherlands and the United States of Indonesia; this union was to take effect by January 1, 1949.

A Brief For Indonesia's Independence²

Mr. Chairman. As slogan to what I am now going to say I would like to apply words which I quote with pleasure from the Netherlands' aide-memoire to the republican government, namely, "seek for that which unites and not for that which divides." After the government's statement of yesterday I shall do this with less pleasure than I had previously envisioned.

It would have been desirable if this declaration had made a small step, even only in intent, toward seeking for that which unites and not toward that which divides. Meanwhile I shall continue to seek for that which unites.

If, however, I shall thereby say things that do not sound pleasant to many Dutchmen, I only mean to clarify how my republican compatriots see things. If one is not well informed about this, then "seeking for that which unites," will not produce the desired results.

I feel the need here to point out right away that by the frightening difficulties arising between the Netherlands and the republic, the military argument, at any rate the overt and covert threat of military force, has not been an indication of "seeking for that which unites."

Had the United States and England failed to intervene, I wonder whether the Netherlands armed forces would not already have made a start with the march to Jogja,³ longingly looked forward to everyday, according to, for instance, a paper like *Trouw*.⁴

Mr. Chairman! That the Dutch used the argument of military force, although indirectly yet nonetheless real, by the deliberations between the Netherlands and the republic, I do not merely consider it bad because one no longer sought for that which unites. But I consider much worse that thereby thoughtlessly one deviated from the right direction leading to the desired, lasting voluntary cooperation.

Mr. Chairman! You must agree with me that voluntary cooperation, which also must be lasting, cannot be obtained by military force unless those forced are, in comparison with the forcer, by far the weaker. England, for instance, could indeed force South Africa to lasting cooperation because South Africa (when it suffered defeat by all- powerful England at the turn of the twentieth century) could only rebuild and develop its resources in cooperation with England.

In Indonesia this is different. At present this country may lose militarily to the Netherlands, but it possesses potential possibilities, which will make it before long as strong as, or even stronger than, the Netherlands. Under such circumstances no one will let himself be forced into a lasting cooperation with the forcer.

The worst is, however, that employing the military argument even indirectly by saber rattling, one consciously omitted a stage provided by the Linggadjati procedure—namely, arbitration. Article 17, section two of the Linggadjati Agreement states verbatim:[5]

> The Dutch Government and the Government of the Republic will submit to arbitration all differences (all differences, Mr. Chairman!) which may arise out of this agreement and which cannot be solved in conference between the two delegations. In such a case the conference will be supplemented by a chairman of another nationality who will have a deciding vote and who will be appointed by the delegates in joint consultation or, if no agreement can be reached, by the President of the High Court of Justice.

Obviously this is explicit enough, Mr. Chairman. As soon as the Netherlands uses the argument of military force even before the question of arbitration has come to order, or worse with deliberate negation of arbitration required under the Linggadjati Agreement, then it acts outside of the agreement and thereby lacks the right to reproach the negotiating partner in the agreement, when that partner makes the same mistake. And certainly the Netherlands lacks the right to use military force, when the republican deviation of the Linggadjati Agreement—if this republican mistake, and I call it a mistake—followed a Dutch deviation, which is also a mistake.

It is appropriate to point this out, because (as is evident from the latest government explanation and the Dutch notes) the Dutch objections are based on the republic's circumvention of the Linggadjati Agreement or violation of it. This is advanced with some petulance of tone and with a final threat of military force.

Studying the republican notes, they, too, advance the same objection formulated no less vehemently but stated in more subdued phraseology. In seeking for that which unites, I have tried to look for the cause of the mutual recriminations. And then the only explanation for one looking for that which unites is that there exists a frightening difference of interpretation of the Linggadjati Agreement. And I believe I can explain this difference with the following analysis.

The Linggadjati Agreement was agreed upon by the negotiating partners to accomplish different goals. The Netherlands acted on the basis of its historical rights, or rather its historical duties toward Indonesia, while the republic proceeded from its right of self-determination, or rather its duties of self-determination.

It is understandable that the emphasis here was placed on legal rights. The Netherlands went to the Linggadjati conference with its historic right, and for the Netherlands the de jure recognition of the sovereignty of the Kingdom of the Netherlands is the essence of the Linggadjati Agreement. It is equally understandable that the Netherlands interprets from this standpoint. Indonesia approached Linggadjati via the right of self-determination. For Indonesia the heart of this basic agreement was the de facto recognition of the republic and that the Linggadjati Agreement was an agreement between two equal partners.

It is from this premise that the republic interprets the Linggadjati Agreement. That the Dutch and the republican interpretations do not overlap should not be surprising. It is actually almost obvious that these interpretations are at variance. And mutual accusations of bad faith by the framing of the interpretation is thus out of place.

If by all mistakes made, one cannot accept that, in the explanation of the Linggadjati Agreement, one acted in good faith, then the thought of a permanent voluntary cooperation should be abandoned.

But if this is obvious, how did both parties become so alienated? Mr. Chairman before the signing of the Linggadjati Agreement, both sides tried very hard to meet each other halfway. They wanted to agree and thus the mutual feeling was propitious.

However, after the signing, when the seventeen points needed to be worked out, the Linggadjati Agreement was divided up into smaller problems; both sides assigned specialists to each separate problem, and they each tried to steal a march on the other, and thus one became increasingly estranged. This process, in my opinion, was strengthened by conflicting views of both parties on the silence factor at the negotiations. For the Netherlander interprets: he who keeps silent agrees; but for the Indonesian this signifies: he who keeps silent disagrees. I am convinced that this fact, more than once, has led to misunderstandings at the negotiations.

It turned out to be fatal that the more experienced Dutch delegation successfully managed first to negotiate the economic part of the agreement, namely, Article 14. There are matters which are vital to the republic and which are referred to with the word "immediate," indicating urgency. Article 1, for instance, states that immediately a start must be made to take the necessary steps to add gradually, by mutual agreement, to the republican areas, regions occupied by allied or Dutch troops. Article 16 stipulates that, immediately after the agreement of Linggadjati, both parties will start decreasing their troop strength. The manner and timing of the reduction, which should commence forthwith, would be subject to agreement.

Yet Article 14, in which the word "immediate" does not occur was first discussed. The republican Minister of Information,[6] made a futile effort to dispel the displeasure this evoked in the republic, by proposing to place officials of the ministry in Surabaya, Semarang, and Bandung, in cooperation with the Netherlands Indies information service to provide advice in the preparation for the gradual inclusion of these cities into the republican area; this was in vain, because military authorities declared this unacceptable, although the proposal had already been approved by Dr. van Mook himself.[7]

One should further take into account that during the already difficult negotiations, shipment of troops from the Netherlands took place, after the signing of Linggadjati, without any, to the Indonesians noticeable, reduction of troops.

Additionally it became known that the KNIL was recruiting troops from Menado and Ambon. The Netherlands army in Indonesia changed from a defensive to an offensive weapon and was felt as a real threat by the Indonesians. Many thought that the Indonesian delegation was required to negotiate with a pistol pointed to its heart. This was even less acceptable because one considered that the Dutch increase in troops, after the signing of the Linggadjati Agreement, was a violation of the basic agreement.

I was in Jogjakarta when the news came that, after the signing of the Linggadjati Agreement, the steamer *Sloterdijk* had left the Netherlands for Indonesia with more than a thousand men. The effect was devastating. I am not exaggerating when I declare that thereby the Linggadjati Agreement was rejected by large groups within the republic, who had been won over after an extensive and laborious campaign by the republican government.

It is this military threat, clearly contrary to the spirit and letter of the agreement, which made the republican government, also against the spirit and letter of the agreement, enter into foreign relations to strengthen as much as possible its own position in case the Dutch army would fly at the republic's throat.

The navy blockade also annoys the republic. This blockade not only hampers exports but imports as well. Motorized tractors are a matter of life and death for the rebuilding in the republican territory. This blockade does not permit the importation of trucks, cars, car tires, car parts, and so forth. The importation of medicine is prohibited by the Dutch military high command. The fact that, in the republic, major operations have taken place without anesthesia demonstrates the gravity of the situation.

Is it then so surprising, Mr. Chairman, that the republic counters the Netherlands blockade with the so-called rice blockade? Mr. Chairman! Permit the import of motors and parts and medicine and the rice blockade is guaranteed to come to an end.

The formation of states in the Malino area took place in a manner not only unsatisfactory to the republic but to many in the Malino area itself and impedes negotiations after the signing of the Linggadjati Agreement.[8]

I understand completely the standpoint of the Netherlands Indies Government; I do not doubt the good intentions and the conviction that in this formation of states the Netherlands Indies Government worked within the framework of the Linggadjati Agreement.

Yet I would appreciate if this high body listened to the republican arguments, which at the same time are the arguments of many in the Malino areas. They are based on Article 2 of the Linggadjati Agreement which states:

> The Netherlands Government and the Government of the Republic will cooperate toward the prompt formation of a sovereign state, named the United States of Indonesia, founded upon the principle of federation.

Thus it is stated that the government of the Netherlands and that of the republic will cooperate toward that goal. If one wants to establish a well functioning federal state, then it is not only desirable but even imperative that each of these states, particularly those to be established, are made ready for that federation. The spirit of Article 2 requires that not only the Netherlands but also the republic takes part in the establishment of these states. The republic accuses the Netherlands Indies Government that, by the building of states undertaken unilaterally, it thinks more about the conflict existing between the republic and itself, rather than the viability of the future United States of Indonesia.

It has built up the state of East Indonesia and the area of West Borneo largely with those population groups, which, in the conflict between the Netherlands and the republic, are more in agreement with the Netherlands than with the republic. The groups more sympathetic to the republic were virtually excluded.

Mr. President. I aver that this way of operating is very understandable, but I cannot agree that this is the right procedure for the formation of states, which on January 1, 1949 together with the republic, must form a federation. This way of establishing states constitutes in advance a source of conflict which, from the start, will hamper the smooth functioning of the federation that is to be established.

Mr. Chairman, is it then so surprising that this way of operating is considered a violation of Article 2 of the Linggadjati Agreement? Is it then so strange that the republic and influential groups in the Malino area desire, on the basis of Article 2, that the Netherlands in cooperation with the republic establishes the united states.

I have talked with the important representatives of Borneo, who assured me that they only accept Kalimantan (Borneo) as a state, if it is established in the way in which they interpret the Linggadjati Agreement, namely, in joint cooperation with the Netherlands and the republic. Fine, one can say, but the state of East Indonesia was already established before the Linggadjati Agreement was signed. The answer to that is: indeed, but the establishment took place after the agreement was reached and at least the spirit of the agreement existed.[9] And what could have been the objection, in the spirit of Article 2, to include the Republic after the signing?

The military and political excesses, which in particular took place in December 1946 and January–February, 1947, might not have been prevented, because the signing took place only at the end of March. However, certainly the present state of war in Celebes and on the island of Bali could have been stopped.

Mr. Chairman. A short time ago I had the pleasure to spend two weeks in Macassar, where I could confidentially and at length speak with practically all of the members of the parliament of East Indonesia. The state of war has caused a radicalization of many of the politically conscious, also of those who are favorably disposed toward the Netherlands, which should give the Netherlands food for thought. One must carefully consider that every radicalization, whether in the republic or in the Malino regions, will inevitably turn against the Netherlands. That the state of war radicalizes was even noticeable among several members of the parliament of East Indonesia.

Besides it is good that one knows in the Netherlands that the organization which must assure and maintain law and order is at the same time the cause of the loss of law and order. The army in the South Celebes and Bali deliberately treated banditry and radical nationalism on an equal basis, often in such a way that evoked shame in every decent human being. This army is simultaneously a threat to law and order.

I have posed the following question to authorities and members of parliament in Macassar of the extreme right and extreme left. If South Celebes were given a batallion of good TRI troops to insure law and order will they succeed better than the KNIL troops?[10] Without exception the answer was "guaranteed!"

I would like to conclude this elaborate digression on South Celebes with an inquiry in conjuction with a question already asked by a member of my party, Professor Logeman, on the events in South Celebes. Is the minister willing to promote that the commission that is presently investigating the political and military excesses (which have a marked political basis) will also examine the prohibition of the political party, the PNI?[11] The important argument for this proscription was that the South Celebes council would have advised this.

Mr. Chairman. I have seen evidence that the South Celebes council, when discussing the PNI case (based on the accusations of the council's chairman), has advised not to proscribe the PNI.[11] This is a matter of great importance for East Indonesia and the leaders of the PNI are, as I am, looking forward to an impartial investigation.

Mr. Chairman. All I have previously broached—the shipment of troops, the blockade, the formation of states and its implications—all this has greatly influenced the republic's action after the signing of the Linggadjati Agreement, the attitude of those trying to sway the political views within the republic. It is inevitable that it has prejudiced the opinion of the republican negotiators and the course of the deliberations with the Dutch delegations.

That the Dutch delegation has been offended by the mistakes of the republic, I shall be the last to deny and condemn. Even the republic is the work of humans, has shortcomings, and makes mistakes which could and may be taken amiss.

Add to this that the Netherlands, at a certain moment, came to the conclusion that it was in monetary straits and therefore under great time pressure; then it is understandable that the parties have become increasingly alienated. Tempers were short, mutual irritability arose, and grievances and recriminations were exchanged.

In this atmosphere, in this light must be regarded the exchange of memos between the delegations and later between the governments. And, in considering this exchange of notes, if one does not confine oneself to basic problems, one will inevitably get lost. It is tempting to examine and discuss the details one by one, but time will not permit this. It is necessary, however, to say something about the famed five points in which the Dutch have summed up the basic issue. I shall do this at the end of my speech.

What I shall now scrutinize is the accusation directed against the republic: that it has violated the Linggadjati Agreement and thus the Netherlands is justified in using force. I would immediately like to emphasize that this procedure was certainly not stipulated in the Linggadjati Agreement. Where and when did the republic violate, after the signing, the agreement? This took place when it made attempts to enter into foreign relations, by bypassing the Linggadjati Agreement. However, one should know that these attempts were caused by a violation of Article 16 of the agreement which required immediate mutual reduction of troop strength, yet the Dutch troop strength, after the signing of the agreement was reinforced by shipment and recruitment.

The Dutch error evoked the republican error. Fine, is the reply, but the official republican reply clearly circumscribes the Linggadjati Agreement. I, too, am of the opinion that this is indeed true, although at the end of my speech I shall elaborate on this; but who can maintain, Mr. Chairman, that the first note of the commissioner-general to which the denounced reply was an answer, who dares to maintain that this Dutch note itself remained within the limits of the Linggadjati Agreement.

The tone, the final and uncompromising character, the threat of military force, not described in the note itself but advanced by the delivery of the note, all this brought the Dutch proposals from the realm of negotiations into the realm of force. The note concerned the Linggadjati Agreement but went beyond it for, in fact in Article 17, the second paragraph referred to the possible differences of interpretation to arbitration. Besides, the note considers reduction of troops only after Dutch demands have been met and thus evades the agreement and violates Article 16, which requires immediate troop withdrawal. This is also circumventing the agreement. In demanding a joint police force, the note, in my opinion, bypasses the Linggadjati Agreement, because it affects the de facto position of the republic recognized in Article 1.

Mr. Chairman. Naturally I do not wish to extenuate the republic's circumvention of the agreement, but I do intend to argue that, when the Netherlands itself made (and started) this mistake, they are not justified in reproaching the republic, and, thereby advance the argument of military force.

Mr. Chairman. The extreme pressures exerted on the republic by England and the United States of America, the threat of a Dutch offensive, and not to forget the knowledge of our Indonesian leaders that the political situation in the Netherlands is such that it cannot generate a policy which completely satisfies the demands that the republic considers legitimate, these three factors put the republic before the choice: bend or burst on the Netherlands government's five demands formulated as an ultimatum.

The republic bent on four of the points, on the fifth it is willing to burst. In my opinion the republic was wise accepting the four points. You may be assured that it was a very difficult decision. Whoever has perused the famed secret minutes of the negotiations in Batavia must concede that the Indonesian, on the first point, has defended and understood that the de facto recognition would lead to the establishment of an interim government, as advanced in its reply note of June 8.

I reject every accusation of bad faith. . . .

I completely agree that differences of opinion are possible on the question of whether the republican interpretation fits into the framework of the Linggadjati Agreement, but I think arbitration is in order here.

I shall admit that I personally believe that on point 1, in an arbitrated decision, the Netherlands interpretation has a better chance of recognition and confirmation than has the Indonesian interpretation. But then the question becomes urgent why here the stage of arbitration required by the Linggadjati Agreement was deliberately bypassed. The agreement does not make provisions for rejection of arbitration based on technical problems. It requires simple arbitration by differences in interpretation.

On the second point dealing with foreign relations, I would like to make a marginal note in the form of a question. If I am not mistaken the interim government of India already could establish in the transition period, thus in time of British sovereignty, foreign relations by mutual exchange of the chargé d'affaires. I believe the Netherlands had already appointed a diplomatic representative for India, namely, Ambassador Lamping. It appears to me Mr. Chairman, that by the establishment and further development of the interim government of Indonesia such a position should be considered. I would very much appreciate hearing the esteemed minister's opinion.

On the effort of the republic to enter into diplomatic relations with other powers, I would like to remark that these efforts were the results of endeavors of the republic to seize every opportunity to strengthen its own position against the threatening attack of the Netherlands armed forces in Indonesia which, and I emphasize this, circumvented the Linggadjati Agreement after the signing of the agreement by the arrival of troops from the Netherlands and from the Minahassa and Ambon.[12]

I would like to comment as follows on the third point regarding the federal institutions: If the republic was convinced that a possible representative of the separate states from the Malino area indeed could by considered representative of those population groups which have directed themselves more toward the republic than toward the Netherlands—and these groups are much larger than one here assumes—then they would undoubtedly have had fewer objections against the precursors of the federal bodies, as projected in the first Dutch note. If the report on the expected composition of the interim government is correct—we have had a chance to read this in yesterday's evening papers and today's morning papers—then the objections, in my opinion, were justified.

I can only express my joy that on point four agreement was reached. Now finally point five. Here the republic rejects the by the Netherlands' demanded joint police force. In the first place, no mention whatever is made in the Linggadjati Agreement of a joint police force. Secondly it is clear that thereby the de facto position of the republic is affected. Thirdly, in many instances a white police force in republican territory during the transition period—when the mutually swept-up nationalist sentiments must be subdued—would be more provoking than protecting.

It would be good if the Dutch and republican governments could come together on the basis of seeking that which unites. This would be a wise policy. It should be encouraged on psychological grounds because it is not advisable for the desired cooperation that one of the partners starts with a complete surrender. This can only hamper lasting cooperation. It is also questionable whether the manner in which the republic was forced to accept the first four points is the best guarantee for a lasting cooperation. I very much doubt this although I do not wish to say that I can no longer see, in this situation, a possibility for a permanent cooperation. I mean, Mr. Chairman, that this is still possible, but—and I speak here as an Indonesian—then the Netherlands must be aware that it must win and not force the Indonesians. Two things must be done:

1) Reduction, as speedily as possible, of Netherlands troop strength in Indonesia in such a way that it is no longer regarded as a threat by the Indonesians, concomitant naturally with Indonesian troop reduction.

2) Entrust the task the Netherlands has to perform in Indonesia to progressive Netherlanders. . . .

Mr. Chairman. I would like to conclude my address by posing some questions and expressing a wish.

More than once the Dutch note emphasized the central authority. Is hereby meant the federal council or the representative of the crown with deciding powers?

Moreover could the esteemed minister outline what, in his opinion, will be the de facto position of the republic within the framework of the de facto, . . . interim government and the de jure position of the representative of the crown?

And finally, Mr. Chairman, I believe that by the establishment of an interim government, the Netherland Indies Government will naturally cease to exist. On this I would appreciate a confirmation of the esteemed minister.

And finally my wish, Mr. Chairman.

In the government's explanation, eight demands resembling an ultimatum are formulated. Four must be met immediately, the other four must be met very shortly. I do not wish to speak on these demands, because the republic still needs to answer these and I wish to spare my fellow countrymen the possibility of hampering their work.

But I do wish the republican government sagacity, taking into account the existing power position, although these do not satisfy their own sense of justice.

To the Netherlands government I also wish sagacity, taking into account not only existing but future power positions, which will influence a lasting voluntary cooperation—which I am hoping for is—and which ultimately should be the Netherlands' goal.

NOTES

1. C. Smit, *Het Akkoord van Linggadjati: Uit het Dagboek van Professor Dr. Ir. W. Schermerhorn* (Amsterdam: Elsevier, 1959). This book, based on the diary of the commission chairman Professor Schermerhorn, gives a good account of the political problems confronting the commission. It is critical of the government's policy toward Indonesia. Charles Wolf, Jr., *The Indonesia Story* (New York: John Day, 1948) gives a fairly impartial account of the problems, but is somewhat favorable to the Dutch position.
2. Kingdom of the Netherlands, Staten Generaal, Tweede Kamer, *Handelingen, 1946/47*, pp. 2065-2068. Discussion on the government's explanation of its policy toward the Netherlands Indies, July 11, 1947.
3. Jogja was the capital of the republic from November, 1945 until December, 1949.
4. *Trouw* was a Dutch conservative Protestant newspaper published in Amsterdam.
5. C. Smit, *Het Akkoord van Linggadjati*, p. 63; Wolf, *op. cit.*, p. 178.
6. The Minister of Information was M. Natsir.
7. Dr. H. J. van Mook was Lieutenant Governor-General of the Netherlands Indies from 1945 until 1948.
8. The Malino Conference was held in July, 1946 and planned to lay the groundwork for a federal structure of Indonesia. Parties present were: the Netherlands Indies Government, and representatives from Borneo, East Indonesia, Bangka, Biliton, and the Riouw archipelago. The conference was labeled a "puppet show" by the republic, which was not invited. Goal of the meeting was to form a United States of Indonesia, whereby each state would possess the greatest possible autonomy. Alastair M. Taylor, *Indonesian Independence and the United Nations* (Ithaca: Cornell University Press, 1960), p. 27.
9. The Linggadjati Agreement was initialled on November 15, 1946; the new state of East Indonesia was created by the Dutch-sponsored conference in Den Pasar, Bali on December, 1946, Taylor, *Indonesian Independence*, p. 28.

10. KNIL (Royal Dutch Indies Army) had many Ambonese and Menadonese recruits. These groups had traditionally been very loyal to the colonial government.
11. PNI (Partai Nasional Indonesia) was founded right after the declaration of independence and was quite influential in the early stages of the republic's existence.
12. As stated previously Ambonese and Menadonese made up a considerable part of the Dutch Indies army.

Glossary

Adat	Custom
Ahimsa	Indian doctrine of nonviolence
Banteng	Wild buffalo
Berkah	Blessing, favor
Bupati	Regent
Bini-dapur	Kitchen wife, sort of backstreet wife
Controleur	Comptroller, lowest rank in the Dutch civil administration
Desa	Village
Djaksa	Public prosecutor
Djawa Kromo	High Javanese Language
Djawa Ngoko	Low Javanese Language
Doctorandus	Academic title indicating a person has completed all requirements for a doctorate except the dissertation.
Doktor Djawa	Native physician, literally Javanese doctor
Geprikkelde stemming	Irritable mood
Grondtoon	Basis, prevailing principle
Hadji	One who has made the pilgrimage to Mecca
Hoofd (en)	Chief(s), here meaning regent(s)
Hoofddjaksa	Chief public prosecutor
Hormat	Respect, honor
Indo	Eurasian
Ingenieur	A degree in engineering
Inlander	Native, this word was used to denote every Indonesian
Irritant gepraat	Irritating talk
Kampong	(Living) Quarter in a city where the village atmosphere prevails

Kebupaten	Regency
Ksatrya	Noble knight of Javanese mythology
Landraad	Civil court for natives
Lotsverbondenheid	United by fate
Lumbung desa	Rice barn for the whole village
Lunak	Meek, gentle
Macht	Power
Magang	Clerk
Mandur	Foreman, overseer
Mantri	Supervisor
Marhaens	All the poor people in Indonesia
Massale Actie	Large-scale action
Menjam (Kemenjam)	Incense
Merdeka	Free, independent
Overheerser	Dominator, alien ruler
Pantun	Quatrain
Patih	Vice-regent
Penghulu	Village chief, Moslem leader
Pustaka	Heirloom
Resident	Dutch administrator in rank below governor
Sana and sini	There and here. Meaning the enemies and the friends of the nationalist movement.
Sawah	Wet-terraced rice field
Sembah	Respectful greeting
Stambul	European theater adapted to Indonesian audiences
Sunnah (sonna)	Tradition and custom of the Prophet accepted as proper conduct for Moslems
Tani	Peasant
Technisch-politieke Term	Technical term used in politics
Tida tau adat (Tidak tahu adat)	Not knowing custom
Ulama	Moslem scholar
Wedono	Indonesian administrative official in rank under the Vice regent *(patih)*
Zakat	One of the five religious requirements for Moslems: the bringing of monetary offers for religious purposes

Suggested Reading

Benda, Harry J. *The Crescent and the Rising Sun. Indonesian Islam under the Japanese Occupation, 1942-1945.* The Hague and Bandung: Van Hoeve, 1958.
Benda, Harry J. and Ruth T. McVey, eds. *The Communist Uprisings of 1926-1927 in Indonesia: Key Documents.* Cornell Modern Indonesia Project, Translation Series. Ithaca, New York, 1960.
Burger, D. H. *Structural Changes in Javanese Society. The Village Sphere and the Supra-Village Sphere.* Cornell Modern Indonesia Project, Translation Series. Ithaca, New York, 1957.
Dahm, Bernhard. *Sukarno and the Struggle for Indonesian Independence.* Translated from the German by Mary F. Somers Heidhues. Ithaca: Cornell University Press, 1969.
_____. *History of Indonesia in the Twentieth Century.* Translated from the German by P. S. Falla. London and New York: Praeger, 1971.
Furnivall, John S. *Netherlands India: A Study of Plural Economy.* New York: MacMillan, 1944.
Geertz, Clifford. *The Religion of Java.* Glencoe, Illinois: The Free Press, 1960.
Kahin, George McT. *Nationalism and Revolution in Indonesia.* Ithaca: Cornell University Press, 1952.
Kartini, Raden Adjeng. *Letters of a Javanese Princess.* Translated from the Dutch by Agnes Louise Symmers. New York: Norton, 1964.
Legge, J. D. *Sukarno: A Political Biography.* London: Allan Lane, 1972.
McVey, Ruth T. *The Rise of Indonesian Communism.* Ithaca: Cornell University Press, 1965.
Palmier, Leslie. *Indonesia and the Dutch.* London: Oxford University Press, 1962.
Sartono Kartodirdjo. *Protest Movements in Rural Java. A Study of Agrarian Unrest in the Nineteenth and Twentieth Century.* Singapore: Oxford University Press, 1973.
Schrieke, B. J. O. *Indonesian Sociological Studies.* 2 vols. The Hague and Bandung: Van Hoeve, 1957.

Sjahrir, Soetan. *Out of Exile*. New York: John Day, 1949.
Soedjatmoko. *An Approach to Indonesian History: Toward an Open Future*. Cornell Modern Indonesia Project, Translation Series. Ithaca, New York, 1958.
Sukarno. *An Autobiography as told to Cindy Adams*. New York: Bobbs Merrill, 1965.
―――. *Toward Freedom and Dignity of Man*. Djakarta: Department of Foreign Affairs, 1961.
Taylor, Alastair M. *Indonesian Independence and the United Nations*. Ithaca: Cornell University Press, 1960.
Van Niel, Robert. *The Emergence of the Modern Indonesian Elite*. The Hague: Van Hoeve, 1960.

Index

Abendanon, J. H., 47
Adams, Cindy, 160n
Ahimsa, 166
Algemene Middelbare School. *See* AMS
Alhamsjah, St. Rais, 63n, 110n, 130n
Ali, Pangeran, 88
Ambon, 45, 56, 184, 189n
Ambonese, 45, 46, 56, 192
AMS (Algemene Middelbare School), 40, 109
Apituley, Dr. H. D. J., 46

Baud, J. C., 36, 42n
BB (Binnenlandsch Bestuur), 24, 36, 39, 41, 170
Bebel, August, 168
Benda, Harry J., ix, x, 62
Berg, L. M. C. van den, 5n
Bergemeier, P., 39
BFO (Bijeenkomst Federaal Overleg), 157n
Bhinneka Tunggal Ika, xvii
Binnenlandsch Bestuur. *See* BB
Bijeenkomst Federaal Overleg. *See* BFO
Blankenstein, Dr. J. van, 118, 141
Bosch, Commissioner General J. van den, 31
Blumberger, J. T. Petrus, 46n, 71n, 131n
British India, 165, 166
Budi Utomo, xiv, 95, 145

Capellen, Governor-General van der, 30
Chiang Kai-shek, 119
Chinese, 21, 55, 73
College of Delegates, 97n

Colonial policy, 4, 27, 138
Council of the Indies, 3, 18
Christian, xviii, 66, 67, 68, 79
Coolie Legislation, 74, 79
Cooperation, 85, 133–136, 139, 143, 145, 152, 154, 163
Cultivation system, 6n, 30, 31

Dahm, Bernhard, 160n
Darna Kusuma, 134
Demak, xiv, 34, 36
Deventer, C. Th. van, 3n
Dewantoro, Ki Hadjar, xiv, xix, 111
Djajadiningrat, Achmad, 17, 18, 27, 73, 147n
Djajadiningrat, Hassan, 23, 24
Djojopuspito, Suwarsi, 115n
Doktor djawa, 12, 45, 47, 48, 49, 52–59
Dutch parliament, 6, 99, 140, 143, 175, 176, 179

East India Company, xiii, 29, 30
East Indonesia, 186–187
Education, xiv, xviii, 3, 4, 6, 7, 8, 10–17, 36–37, 46, 51, 111–114
Effendi, Rustam, 99, 175
Ensiklopedia Indonesia, 4
Ethical policy, xivn, 4, 147
Eurasians (Indos), xixn, 52, 59n
Exhorbitant rights, 85, 140

Fatherland Club (Vaderlandsche Club), 87, 97n
Feber Amendment, 143, 147n

Federspiel, Howard M., 110n
Fock, Governor-General D., xiv, 133, 135, 139, 143, 147

Gabungan Politik Indonesia. *See* GAPI
Gandhi, Mahatma, 166, 168
GAPI (Gabungan Politik Indonesia), 62, 65, 121, 122n
Gokhale, Gopal Krishna, 114
Graaff, S. de, xv, 74, 81n
Graeff, Governor-General A. de, xv, 83, 86, 133, 138, 139, 141, 142, 144, 146, 147
Gunawan, R. Mangunkusumo, 23

Hadiningrat, Pangeran Ario, xiv, xvii, 3, 4, 15n
Harahap, Parada, 109
Hassan, A., 110
Hasselman, C. J., 6n
Hatta, M., xv, xvii, xixn, 85, 129, 131
HBS (Hogere Burger School), xiv, 23, 40
Helsdingen, J. J. van, 24
Heijting, H. G., 81n
H.I.K. (Hollandsch Inlandsche Kweekschool), 109, 112, 113
H.I.S. (Hollandsch Inlandsch School), 112
Hogere Burger School. *See* HBS
Holst, Henriette Roland Holst, 165, 173n
Hoofdenscholen (Training school for native officials), 8, 12, 14n, 15n, 31, 36, 40
Hugo, Victor, 79, 82n
Hurgronje, C. Snouck, xiv, xixn, 4, 17, 42n, 61, 63n, 66, 68, 70, 71, 71n

Indische Gids, 3, 15n, 58n
Indisch Genootschap, 42n, 47
Indonesia Merdeka, 129, 139
Indonesian Independence, xvi, 46, 86, 130, 138, 146, 149, 150, 151, 160, 181
Indonesian parliament (Indonesia Berparlamen), 62, 85, 121
Iskandar Dinata, Oto, 170, 173n
Islam, 21, 61, 62, 65-67, 68, 70, 71, 77-78, 110

Japan, 86, 119, 176, 177n
Japanese occupation, 62, 109, 110, 151, 179
Java War, 30, 31
Javanese, low, 9, 15n
Jonghe, Governor-General B. de, xv, 86n
Juynboll, T. W., 67

Kahin, George McTurnan, 157n
Kaliurang, 153
Kartini, Raden Adjeng, 3
Kasimo, 121, 125

Kesteren, C. E. van, 3
Killearn, Lord, 179
Koch, D. M. G., 63n, 86n, 120, 122n
Kohlbrugge, J. H. F., 47
KNIL (Koninklijk Nederlands Indies Leger), 104, 105, 184, 187
Kesatrya, 125, 125n
Kusuma Sumantri, 92
Kusumo Utoyo, 88, 89, 145

Lapian, 104-107, 107n
League against Imperialism and Colonial Oppression, 129
League of Young Moslems (Jong Islamieten Bond), 65, 66, 67, 70, 71
Levelt, H. J., 120, 122n
Linggadjati Agreement, 151, 179, 182-190, 191n

Malino, 185, 189
Mangkubumi (Hamengku Buwono), 162, 164n
Mangkurats (Amangkurats) 162, 164n
Marx, Karl, 171
Marhaen, 167, 168, 173n
Meer Uitgebreid Lager Onderwijs. *See* MULO
Menado, 175, 184
Menadonese, 175
Minangkabau, 61, 109, 129
Mochtar, 88
Mogot, 121, 125
Moluccas Political Alliance, 46
Mook, H. J. van, 184
Moslem, 61, 62, 65, 66, 67, 82n
Muhammadijah, 95, 111
MULO (Meer Uitgebreid Lager Onderwijs), 112

Nationalist faction, 87, 88, 97n
Nationalist movement, 4, 117, 145
Natsir M., xvii, xixn, 109-110, 117, 191n
Negarakrtagama, 28
Nehru, J., 129, 166
Netherlands government, 182, 188
Netherlands Indies government, 185, 190, 191
Netherlands Indies Liberal League, 18
Niewenhuis, G. J., 114
Nja Arif, 88
Noncooperation, xv, xvi, xvii, 133-136, 143, 165-167, 169-172
Noor, Tadjuddin 121, 125

Palar, L. N., 175, 176, 177n
Partai Nasional Indonesia. *See* PNI

Partai Sosialis Indonesia. *See* PSI
Partai Perempuan Indonesia, 95
Pasundan, 95, 173n
Penal Sanction, xixn, 18, 19n, 73–81, 81n, 163, 164n
Pendidikan Indonesia, 129, 130
Pendidikan Islam, 109
People's Council, xv, xvi, xviii, 18, 22, 73, 81n, 84, 85, 86n, 87, 88, 89, 96n 97n, 99, 101, 104, 105, 107, 107n, 117, 118, 120, 121, 122n, 123, 125, 134, 135, 136, 140, 141, 143, 145, 146, 147n, 148
Pergerakan Penjadar, 62
Perhimpunan Indonesia, 129, 139
Permufakatan Perhimpunan Politik Kebangsaan Indonesia. *See* PPPKI
Persatuan Islam, 109, 110n
Persindo, 75
Philippines, 114, 154
Pluvier, J. M., 101n, 122n
PNI (Partai Nasional Indonesia), 90, 91, 94, 95, 146, 147, 166, 172, 187, 192n
PPPKI (Permufakatan Perhimpunan Politiek Kebangsaan Indonesia), 144, 145, 163, 164n
PSI (Partai Sosialis Indonesia), 146, 166
PUTERA (Pusat Tenaga Rakjat), 62

Raalte, E. N. van, xixn
Reformers, xviii, xix, 43, 95
Regents, xiv, xv, xvii, 3, 4, 11, 13, 17, 28–42
Regency councils, 18, 27, 33–35, 38, 41
Renville principles, 151–153, 156n
Republik Indonesia Serikat, 149, 152, 155
Revolutionaries, xviii, 96, 145
Rivai, Abdul, xvi, 45
Round Table Conference, 149, 152, 155, 156n
Roep, M., 88

Salim, H. A., xvi, xvii, 60–62, 63n, 65, 66
Sarekat Ambon, 46
Sarekat Islam, 21, 22–25, 61, 172
Sarekat Dagang Islam, 21
Schermerhorn, W., 191n
Scherp, Mr., 47, 48
School for Doktor Djawa, xixn, 12, 45, 47, 49, 52
School for Native Physicians. *See* STOVIA
Schrieke, B. J. O., 14n, 42n

Schrieke, J. J., 39
Sjahrir, Sutan, xvi, 85, 130, 157n
Smit, C., 191n
Soangkupon, Abdul, 88, 121, 122
Sosroningrat, 3
Stirum, Governor-General J. P. van Limburg, xvi, 138
Stokvis, J. E., 5n, 81, 81n, 135, 136n, 141, 175
STOVIA (School for Native Physicians), xiv, 59n
Sukawati, Tjokorde Gde Rake, 97n
Sukarno, Ir., xv–xix, xixn, 85, 91, 110, 129, 130, 147, 159, 160, 160n, 163n, 173n
Sutadi, 88
Suroso, 88
Sutardjo Kartohadikusumo, xvii, 99, 100, 106, 121, 122, 122n, 125
Sutardjo Petition, xvii, 62, 85, 99, 100
Sutomo, Raden, xv, 83

Tabrani, M., 85, 109
Taman Siswa, 95, 111
Taylor, Alastair M., 159n, 191n, 196
Teachers' training school, xvii, 112, 113
Tehupeiory, W. K., xviii, 45–47
Tentara Republik Indonesia. *See* TRI
Thamrin, M. H., xv, xvi, xvii, 84, 85, 86, 93, 97n, 103, 107n, 117, 118, 119, 121, 122, 122n, 123, 125, 134, 135, 160
Tjarda van Starkenborgh Stachouwer, A. W. L., xvi, xixn
Tjipto Mangunkusumo, Dr., xiv, xixn, 125, 125n
Tjondronegoro, R. M. A. A., 3
Tjokroaminoto, H. O. S., 21, 159
TRI (Tentara Republik Indonesia), 187

United Nations, 149, 176
United States, 73, 154, 181, 188

Vice regent *(patih)*, 34
Visman Commission, 121, 122n

Wang Ching-wei, 86, 119, 123, 124, 125n
Wal, S. L. van de, 63n, 86, 101n
Wiwoho, Purbohadidjojo, 67, 71n, 122, 122n
Wolf, Charles, Jr., 191n

Zentgraaff, H., 161, 162, 164n

Greta Oosterink Wilson was born in Bandung, Indonesia of Dutch parents. Her father was director of the School for Indonesian Officials and her mother was descended from an old Dutch colonial family in Indonesia.

The author received her B.A. from the University of Amsterdam, M.A. degrees from Columbia University (in history) and Yale University (in Southeast Asian Studies), and a J.D. from the University of California, Davis. She currently resides in Diablo, California.

Asian Studies at Hawaii

No. 1   *Bibliography of English Language Sources on Human Ecology, Eastern Malaysia and Brunei.* Compiled by Conrad P. Cotter with the assistance of Shiro Saito. September 1965. Two parts. (Available only from Paragon Book Gallery, New York.)

No. 2   *Economic Factors in Southeast Asian Social Change.* Edited by Robert Van Niel. May 1968. Out of print.

No. 3   *East Asian Occasional Papers (1).* Edited by Harry J. Lamley. May 1969.

No. 4   *East Asian Occasional Papers (2).* Edited by Harry J. Lamley. July 1970.

No. 5   *A Survey of Historical Source Materials in Java and Manila.* Robert Van Niel. February 1971.

No. 6   *Educational Theory in the People's Republic of China: The Report of Ch'ien Chung-Jui.* Translated by John N. Hawkins. May 1971. Out of print.

No. 7   *Hai Jui Dismissed from Office.* Wu Han. Translated by C. C. Huang. June 1972.

No. 8   *Aspects of Vietnamese History.* Edited by Walter F. Vella. March 1973.

No. 9   *Southeast Asian Literatures in Translation: A Preliminary Bibliography.* Philip N. Jenner. March 1973.

No.10   *Textiles of the Indonesian Archipelago.* Garrett and Bronwen Solyom. October 1973. Out of print.

No.11   *British Policy and the Nationalist Movement in Burma, 1917–1937.* Albert D. Moscotti. February 1974.

No.12   *Aspects of Bengali History and Society.* Edited by Rachel Van M. Baumer. December 1975.

No.13   *Nanyang Perspective: Chinese Students in Multiracial Singapore.* Andrew W. Lind. June 1974.

No. 14 *Political Change in the Philippines: Studies of Local Politics preceding Martial Law.* Edited by Benedict J. Kerkvliet. November 1974.
No. 15 *Essays on South India.* Edited by Burton Stein. February 1976.
No. 16 *The* Caurāsī Pad *of Śrī Hit Harivaṁś.* Charles S. J. White. 1977.
No. 17 *An American Teacher in Early Meiji Japan.* Edward R. Beauchamp. June 1976.
No. 18 *Buddhist and Taoist Studies I.* Edited by Michael Saso and David W. Chappell. 1977.
No. 19 *Sumatran Contributions to the Development of Indonesian Literature, 1920–1942.* Alberta Joy Freidus. 1977.
No. 20 *Insulinde: Selected Translations from Dutch Writers of Three Centuries on the Indonesian Archipelago.* Edited by Cornelia N. Moore, 1978.
No. 21 *Regents, Reformers, and Revolutionaries: Indonesian Voices of Colonial Days, Selected Historical Readings, 1899–1949.* Translated, edited, and annotated by Greta O. Wilson, 1978.

Orders for Asian Studies at Hawaii publications should be directed to The University Press of Hawaii, 2840 Kolowalu Street, Honolulu, Hawaii 96822. Present standing orders will continue to be filled without special notification.